# THE CYCLADES TRAVEL GUIDE

## 2024 Edition

Island-Hopping through the Cyclades: Navigating the Aegean Gem by Gem, from Santorini to Mykonos

## Jim Baxter

All rights reserved. No part of this book may be reproduced, stored in a retrieval system, or transmitted in any form or by any means, electronic, mechanical, photocopying, recording, or otherwise, without the prior written permission of the copyright owner. The information contained in this book is for general information purposes only. The author and publisher make no representations or warranties of any kind, express or implied, about the completeness, accuracy, reliability, suitability or availability with respect to the book or the information, products, services, or related graphics contained in the book for any purpose. Any reliance you place on such information is therefore strictly at your own risk.

Copyright © 2023 by Jim Baxter.

# TABLE OF CONTENT

## *Introduction* _____ 7

### Why Cyclades? Unveiling the Allure and Charm of the Archipelago _____ 9

## *Chapter 1: Planning Your Cyclades Adventure* _____ 13

### Understanding the Cyclades Archipelago: A Map of Islands and Connections _____ 13

### Best Times to Visit: Navigating the Seasons and Crowds ___ 22

### Visa and Entry Requirements: Essential Travel Logistics _26

### Budgeting for the Trip: Accommodation, Transportation, and Daily Expenses _____ 28

## *Chapter 2: Embarking on the Cycladic Odyssey* _____ 37

### Athens as Your Gateway: Arrival and Preparations _____ 37

### Navigating Local Transport: Buses, Taxis, and Rental Services _____ 44

## *Chapter 3: Exploring Cyclades' Jewels* _____ 59

### Santorini: A Caldera of Beauty and Romance _____ 59
- Ancient Akrotiri: Unveiling Santorini's Buried Legacy _____ 61
- Caldera Cruises: Sailing the Romantic Waves _____ 62
- Artistic Inspirations: The Island's Muse _____ 64
- Santorini's Underwater World: A Marine Wonderland _____ 65

### Mykonos: The Glamorous Playground of the Cyclades ___ 67
- Chora's Charm and Iconic Windmills _____ 67
- Beach Clubs, Nightlife, and Beyond _____ 68
- Luxury Shopping and Designer Boutiques: Mykonos' Fashion Haven ___ 69
- Delve into History: Delos Island Excursion _____ 70
- Art and Galleries: Mykonos' Creative Pulse _____ 71
- Celebrity Hotspot and Paparazzi Haven _____ 72
- Wellness and Relaxation Retreats: Finding Serenity Amidst Glamour ___ 73

### Naxos: Where Tradition Meets Tranquility _____ 74
- Naxos Town and Portara: Where the Past Meets Present _____ 74
- Hiking Mount Zeus and Cultural Immersion _____ 75

Windmills and Little Venice: Iconic Landmarks ___78
Panagia Paraportiani: Architectural Marvel ___80
Matogianni Street: Shopping and Strolling ___81
Mykonian Spiti: Culinary and Cultural Experiences ___82

## Paros and Antiparos: A Duo of Delights ___84
Parikia and Naoussa Exploration ___84
Beaches, Caves, and Offbeat Escapes in Antiparos ___85
Artistic Enclaves and Workshops: Nurturing Creativity in Paros and Antiparos ___88
Sunset Sailing and Nautical Adventures: Writing Poetry on the Aegean Waters ___90
Local Festivals and Celebrations: Dancing to the Rhythm of Tradition ___91
Underwater Exploration and Diving: A Symphony of Marine Beauty ___92
Day Trip to Despotiko Island: Unearthing Archaeological Treasures ___92

## Milos: Hidden Treasures in the Cyclades ___94
Sarakiniko's Moon-Like Landscape ___94
Catacombs, Sea Caves, and Sulphur Springs ___95
Milos Mining Museum: Unearthing the Island's Industrial Past ___96
Firopotamos: A Quaint Fishing Village by the Sea ___98
Plaka: Exploring Milos' Enchanting Capital ___100
Ancient Theater of Milos: A Step into the Past ___102
Tsigrado Beach: A Secluded Cove of Tranquility ___104

# *Chapter 4: Soaking in Cycladic Culture and Cuisine* ___107

**Gastronomic Journey: Savoring Authentic Cycladic Delicacies** ___107

**Seafood Specialties and Island-Infused Flavors** ___110

**Must-Try Dishes and Recommended Restaurants** ___113

# *Chapter 5: Activities and Adventures* ___123

**Basking in the Sun: Cyclades' Top Beach Escapes** ___123

**Scenic Hikes and Nature Trails: Exploring the Islands on Foot** ___128

**Water Sports and Marine Adventures: Diving, Snorkeling, and more** ___140

**Connecting with the Past: Archaeological Sites and Historical Tours** ___148

## Chapter 6: Travel Itineraries ___153

Family-Friendly Itineraries in the Cyclades: Crafting Unforgettable Adventures for All Ages ___153

5-Day Travel Itineraries for Exploring the Cyclades___161

7-Day Travel Itineraries for Exploring the Cyclades: Island-Hopping Adventures ___165

## Chapter 7: Practical Tips and Travel Essentials ___181

Currency, Language, and Communication ___181

Staying Safe and Healthy: Medical Facilities and Precautions ___182

Responsible Travel: Navigating Environmental Concerns 183

## Chapter 8: Saying Farewell to the Cyclades ___185

## Appendix: Handy Resources and References ___189

Useful Websites, Apps, and Travel Services: ___189

Glossary of Local Terms and Phrases: ___191

## Important Note Before You Continue Reading

Unlock a World of Wonder: Embrace the Uncharted Beauty of the Cyclades

Step into a realm where extraordinary experiences lie within the pages of this exceptional travel guide. Our mission is simple: to ignite your imagination, fuel your creativity, and awaken the daring adventurer within you. Unlike conventional guides, we choose to forgo images, as we firmly believe in the power of firsthand discovery—unfiltered and uninfluenced by preconceptions. Prepare yourself for an enchanting voyage, where each monument, every corner, and every hidden gem eagerly await your personal encounter. Why spoil the exhilaration of that first glimpse, that overwhelming sense of awe? Get ready to embark on an unparalleled journey, where the vessel propelling you forward is none other than your boundless imagination, and you will be the architect of your own destiny. Abandon any preconceived notions and find yourself transported to an authentic Cycladean experience, a realm teeming with extraordinary revelations. Brace yourself, for the magic of this expedition begins now, and remember, the most breathtaking images will be the ones painted by your own eyes.

In stark contrast to traditional guides, this book rejects the need for detailed maps. Why, you ask? Because we fervently believe that the greatest discoveries occur when you lose yourself, when you surrender to the ebb and flow of your surroundings, and embrace the thrill of the unknown path. No predetermined itineraries, no precise directions—our intention is to liberate you, allowing you to explore the Cyclades on your terms, without boundaries or limitations. Surrender to the currents and unveil hidden treasures that no map could ever reveal. Embrace audacity, follow your instincts, and prepare to be astounded. The magic of this expedition commences in your world without maps, where roads materialize with each step, and the most extraordinary adventures await within the unexplored folds of the unknown.

# Introduction

**Welcome to the Cyclades: An Overview of Greece's Island Paradise**

Close your eyes and imagine the symphony of nature's elements harmonizing in a place of unparalleled beauty. Picture the gentle waves of the Aegean Sea rhythmically caressing the sun-kissed shores, a serenade of nature's embrace. Above, the azure sky stretches endlessly, punctuated by the iconic silhouette of timeless windmills standing like stoic sentinels, a living connection to the past. It's a scene that transcends time and transports you to a realm where beauty and enchantment dance hand in hand - welcome to the Cyclades.

This corner of the world, nestled in the heart of Greece, boasts a collection of over 200 islands that collectively create an archipelago unlike any other. The Cyclades have lured travelers for generations, weaving a tapestry of allure that beckons exploration. It's a place where every twist of the cobblestone streets, every whisper of the sea breeze, and every brushstroke of the setting sun on the horizon creates an experience that resonates deeply within.

As you embark on this journey through the Cyclades, this introduction sets the stage for the adventure that awaits. It's an invitation to step into a world that stretches beyond the physical boundaries of the islands themselves, inviting you to immerse yourself in the essence of Cycladic life.

Imagine setting foot on ancient shores where myths and legends were born, where gods and mortals mingled in tales of heroism and romance. Envision strolling through villages that seem to have emerged from a painter's palette, their whitewashed walls and cobalt domes imbuing every corner with a sense of timelessness.

But this guide isn't just about the picturesque vistas and historical remnants that define the Cyclades. It's about the spirit of exploration, about embracing the unknown with open arms. It's about savoring local delicacies that tantalize your taste buds and learning the stories that shape the islanders' lives.

Through vivid descriptions that evoke the senses, vibrant imagery that captures the essence of each island, and essential context that bridges the past and present, this section creates a symphony of anticipation and wonder. It's the overture to an operatic journey where you, the traveler, take center stage.

So, as you turn the pages of this guide, let the rhythm of the waves, the brilliance of the sunsets, and the echo of ancient tales guide you. Welcome to the Cyclades, where beauty is a way of life, and enchantment is around every corner. Your adventure awaits, and every island is a note in the melody of discovery.

# Why Cyclades? Unveiling the Allure and Charm of the Archipelago

Amidst the myriad travel destinations that grace the globe, the Cyclades stand as a testament to nature's artistry and human history's tapestry. This segment delves into the reasons why the Cyclades hold a special place in the hearts of travelers worldwide, drawing them in like a siren's song.

**Timeless Beauty: A Canvas of Dreams**

Picture yourself standing on a cobblestone alley, the sun casting a warm glow over the iconic whitewashed buildings that dot the landscape. The contrast of pure white against the deep blue sea creates a visual symphony that has stirred the souls of artists, poets, and dreamers for generations. This is the Cyclades' signature beauty, a symphony of light and color that transcends time. From the picturesque villages clinging to hillsides to the romantic sunsets that set the sea ablaze, the Cyclades offer a canvas of dreams that never fades. This allure isn't fleeting; it's a timeless beauty that invites you to step into a world where reality and reverie intertwine.

**Myth and Legend: Echoes of Ancient Tales**

The Cyclades aren't just a collection of islands; they're living pages of ancient mythology and historical significance. Every island has a story to tell, a tale woven into the fabric of its very being. Santorini whispers of the lost city of Atlantis, while Delos resonates with the birthplace of gods and goddesses, like Apollo and Artemis. The labyrinth of Knossos in Crete and the legends of Minos and the Minotaur remind us that beneath the sun-drenched beauty lies a tapestry of stories that have shaped civilizations. The Cyclades are more than a destination; they're a living tableau of ancient tales, beckoning you to walk in the footsteps of heroes and gods.

## Diverse Experiences: Every Island a World of Its Own

The Cyclades are a tapestry woven with diverse threads, each island a world of its own. Whether you seek the vibrant rhythm of Mykonos' nightlife, the untouched tranquility of Milos' hidden beaches, or the timeless elegance of Naxos' ancient ruins, the archipelago offers a medley of experiences that cater to every wanderer's soul. Explore the vibrant alleyways of Paros, where history and artistry converge, or embark on a cultural journey through the Cycladic way of life in serene villages. The islands are not isolated entities but interconnected gems, each offering a unique facet of the Cycladic charm.

## Cultural Immersion: Unveiling Authentic Traditions

Beyond the well-trodden paths, there lies a realm of authentic Cycladic life waiting to be discovered. Engage in local festivals where traditions come alive, be it the religious fervor of Easter celebrations or the lively dance and music festivals that fill the summer air. Delve into the rhythm of everyday life, where locals carry forward customs passed down through generations. This section unveils the vibrant tapestry of Cycladic culture, where you'll find that the islands' true beauty lies not just in their landscapes, but in the hearts of the people who call them home.

## Culinary Delights: A Feast for the Senses

To explore the Cyclades is to embark on a culinary journey that tantalizes the taste buds and feeds the soul. From the catch of the day prepared with traditional recipes to the aromatic herbs that infuse dishes with Cycladic essence, the islands' cuisine is a celebration of nature's bounty. Picture yourself dining by the sea, the salty breeze carrying the aroma of freshly grilled seafood and locally sourced produce. It's not just about sustenance; it's about savoring moments and flavors that encapsulate the very essence of the Cyclades.

Intriguing and immersive, the Cyclades beckon with a symphony of beauty, history, diversity, culture, and culinary wonders. This introduction is your gateway to a journey that will unravel the layers of these islands, inviting you to explore, experience, and embrace the magic that defines the Cycladic way of life.

By exploring the reasons behind the Cyclades' allure, this part of the introduction sparks curiosity and sets the stage for the comprehensive exploration that awaits. As you turn the pages of this guide, you'll uncover the intricacies of island-hopping through this remarkable archipelago, ensuring that your journey through the Cyclades is as fulfilling as it is memorable.

# Chapter 1: Planning Your Cyclades Adventure

## Understanding the Cyclades Archipelago: A Map of Islands and Connections

Nestled in the azure waters of the Aegean Sea, the Cyclades archipelago stands as a captivating constellation of islands, each with its own unique character and allure. Encompassing a total of 24 inhabited islands and numerous smaller islets, the Cyclades derive their name from the Greek word "kyklos," meaning circle, as they seem to form an elegant circular arrangement around the sacred isle of Delos.

### Mapping the Cyclades: An Overview of Island Distribution

Imagine a landscape of sun-kissed islands scattered like precious gems across the Aegean expanse, their stories etched into the very fabric of the sea. The Cyclades archipelago, a masterpiece of nature's artistry, beckons with its harmonious blend of rugged terrains and gentle valleys, each island a unique brushstroke on a canvas of boundless blue. Among these islands, you'll encounter a rich tapestry of experiences, from the sun-soaked beaches to the cobblestone streets of ancient villages.

As you delve into this chapter, prepare to embark on a journey of exploration that transcends geography to unveil the soul of the Cyclades. The landscape of these islands is an embodiment of contrasts – from arid, wind-carved cliffs that rise proudly against the horizon to valleys adorned with olive groves and vineyards that flourish in the embrace of sea breezes.

It's a land where the iconic Cycladic architecture flourishes – white-washed buildings adorned with vivid blue accents, a visual representation of the Cyclades' harmony with the sky and sea. This architecture isn't just about aesthetics; it's a reflection of the practicality of island life, with thick walls that keep interiors cool and an aesthetic that evokes tranquility and timelessness.

**Each Island, a Unique Tale**

Picture the crescent-shaped embrace of Santorini, its dramatic caldera views a testament to the forces of nature that have shaped its evolution. Wander through its narrow alleyways and you'll uncover the stories of a once-thriving volcanic society, preserved in the nooks and crannies of its cliffside settlements.

Then, turn your gaze to Mykonos, a whirlwind of energy and charm. Its vibrant harbors are a playground for those seeking the perfect blend of nightlife and relaxation. Cobalt blue domes punctuate the white-washed expanse, reflecting the island's exuberance against the backdrop of the Aegean's tranquility.

Naxos, on the other hand, is a haven of serene beauty and authenticity. Verdant valleys and rolling hills provide a stark contrast to the arid landscapes of its neighbors. Discover hidden chapels and ancient ruins, relics of a past that still breathes through the island's culture and architecture.

Paros, with its understated elegance, unveils hidden treasures beneath its unassuming façade. Beaches of golden sands beckon, while charming villages resonate with a timeless authenticity. Delve into the island's marble quarries, a testament to the island's historical significance and craftsmanship.

Through rich descriptions and vivid imagery, you'll uncover the heartbeats of these islands – their histories, their present-day charm, and the promise of experiences yet to be embraced. The Cyclades, though united by their proximity, are a symphony of individual melodies, each playing a part in the captivating song of the archipelago.

As you immerse yourself in these island stories, you'll find your own aspirations echoed in their beauty. Whether you seek the tranquility of isolated beaches, the vibrancy of bustling harbors, or the stories etched into ancient stones, the Cyclades offer a spectrum of experiences, waiting to be woven into your own narrative of adventure and discovery.

# Interconnected Islands: Navigating the Ferry System

As you delve deeper into the enchanting world of the Cyclades, you'll soon realize that these islands are not merely isolated paradises, but rather, they are woven together by a network of sea routes that enhance their collective charm. While each Cycladic island is undoubtedly a self-contained paradise with its own unique allure, it is the interplay of these islands – the seamless connections between them – that elevates the archipelago to an extraordinary level of allure.

### *Embarking on Sea Voyages of Anticipation*

Imagine stepping onto a ferry, your excitement palpable as you prepare to leave one stunning island behind and journey toward another. The ferry system is the lifeline that knits these islands together, creating a fascinating tapestry of exploration. The Cycladic ferry experience is more than just a mode of transportation; it's an embodiment of adventure and discovery. With every departure, you're not just leaving a port; you're embarking on a voyage of anticipation, bound for a new island horizon.

### *The Pulse of Island-Hopping*

The ferry system is the pulse of Cycladic island-hopping. It's a rhythmic heartbeat that ensures the archipelago's vitality. This chapter invites you to understand the nuances of this intricate network. Discover the routes that crisscross the

Aegean, connecting bustling harbors to tranquil coves and vibrant towns to serene villages. The Cycladic islands, each with its own character and charm, become nodes in a grand symphony of travel possibilities.

### *High-Speed Marvels and Leisurely Journeys*

The ferry options are as diverse as the islands themselves. For those eager to maximize their exploration time, high-speed ferries offer swift connections between the main hubs. These vessels, sleek and modern, cut through the waves with purpose, allowing you to hop from one paradise to another in a matter of hours. If your heart yearns for a more leisurely experience, the traditional ferries are your ticket to savoring the journey. Their unhurried pace gives you the luxury of time – time to gaze at the horizon, to feel the sea breeze on your skin, and to relish every passing island vista.

### *A Dance with the Aegean*

The ferry journeys aren't just transitions from point A to point B; they're a dance with the Aegean itself. The sunlit waters mirror the vibrant blue skies, merging into a seamless expanse that stretches to the horizon. As you cruise from island to island, the Aegean offers you glimpses of its grandeur – its depths teeming with life, its surface a shimmering masterpiece. It's a sensory immersion that turns every ferry ride into an unforgettable experience, an integral part of your Cycladic adventure.

## *Discovering Beyond the Horizon*

With every departure, a sense of anticipation lingers in the air – the excitement of discovering what lies beyond the horizon. The ferry system transforms the Cyclades from isolated islands into a symphony of experiences. As you traverse the Aegean, the islands' stories unfold before you. And as you approach a new harbor, you're not just arriving at a destination; you're stepping into a narrative waiting to be explored.

In the Cyclades, island-hopping isn't just a journey; it's a way of life, a celebration of the Aegean's vastness and the archipelago's interconnected spirit. So, as you embark on these maritime adventures, embrace the thrill of discovery, the romance of the sea, and the ever-present promise that beyond every island horizon, another treasure of the Cyclades awaits your exploration.

## Transportation Hubs: Athens, Santorini, and Mykonos

As you embark on your Cyclades adventure, three key transportation hubs stand out as gateways to this island paradise: Athens, Santorini, and Mykonos.

## *Athens: The Gateway to Greek Adventure*

The journey to the Cyclades begins in Athens, the historic capital of Greece. The Athens International Airport, known as "Eleftherios Venizelos," stands as a bustling gateway that connects travelers from around the world to the wonders of the Cyclades. Upon arrival, you'll find yourself enveloped in the harmonious blend of ancient grandeur and modern vitality that characterizes this iconic city.

Athens isn't just a logistical starting point; it's a destination rich in historical significance. As you step onto Athenian soil, you're greeted by the echoes of philosophers, warriors, and architects whose legacies have shaped the world. You might choose to immerse yourself in the majesty of the Acropolis, where the Parthenon stands as an enduring symbol of human achievement. Or perhaps you'll stroll through the charming Plaka district, where narrow streets wind through quaint shops and tavernas.

While Athens thrives with millennia of history, it's also a springboard to your Cycladic adventure. From here, you can seamlessly transition to the next phase of your journey—whether that involves exploring the Cyclades' maritime wonders, soaking in the island life, or embarking on a domestic flight to one of the key Cycladic airports.

### *Santorini: The Mesmerizing Gem of the Aegean*

Santorini, often referred to as the "jewel of the Aegean," beckons with its captivating beauty and dramatic landscapes. The Santorini Airport serves as a crucial link between the mainland and this stunning island destination. Arriving at the airport, you'll immediately sense the allure of this Cycladic paradise—the promise of breathtaking sunsets, pristine white-washed buildings, and the deep blue waters of the caldera.

Santorini's volcanic history has bestowed it with a distinctive charm. The caldera's steep cliffs reveal layers of history etched in the rock formations. The island's iconic villages, such as Oia and Fira, appear as if they've emerged from the sea, cascading down the hillsides in a picturesque symphony of architecture. As you explore the labyrinthine streets, you'll encounter art galleries, boutique shops, and tavernas that tantalize the senses.

Beyond its visual splendor, Santorini offers a glimpse into the Cyclades' unique culture and traditions. You'll have the opportunity to savor local delicacies, indulge in wine-tasting experiences, and partake in festivals that celebrate the island's heritage. Santorini also serves as a vital hub for onward travel within the Cyclades, making it an essential stop for those embarking on island-hopping adventures.

## *Mykonos: Where Cosmopolitan Energy Meets Island Serenity*

Mykonos, a cosmopolitan haven renowned for its vibrant nightlife and captivating beaches, beckons travelers seeking a perfect blend of relaxation and excitement. Mykonos Island National Airport welcomes flights from numerous international locations, ensuring convenient access to this Cycladic gem. From the moment you set foot on the island, you'll be swept up in the effervescent energy that defines Mykonos.

The island's allure lies not only in its golden beaches and turquoise waters but also in its lively ambiance. Mykonos is famed for its bustling nightlife, where beachfront bars and clubs come alive as the sun sets. Chora, the island's main town, exudes charm with its narrow alleys, white-washed buildings, and iconic windmills.

Mykonos isn't just about its lively scene, though. It offers a balance between excitement and tranquility. You can explore quiet corners, sunbathe on pristine beaches, and immerse yourself in the Cycladic way of life. As a transportation hub, Mykonos provides a convenient starting point for your island-hopping journey, allowing you to set sail for other Cycladic treasures.

These transportation hubs serve not only as logistical foundations but also as entrancing introductions to the Cyclades' magic. They mark the starting points of your adventure and offer seamless connections to the islands, ensuring that your journey is as enchanting as the destinations themselves.

In conclusion, the Cyclades archipelago is a tapestry of beauty, culture, and history woven by the Aegean's gentle waves. With a deep understanding of the island distribution, the ferry system, and the pivotal transportation hubs, you'll be empowered to craft an island-hopping odyssey that resonates with your desires. Each ferry ride becomes a bridge between your dreams and the vibrant reality of the Cyclades, where white-washed villages, turquoise waters, and captivating experiences await your arrival.

# Best Times to Visit: Navigating the Seasons and Crowds

### Choosing the Perfect Time to Explore the Cyclades: A Seasonal Journey

Selecting the ideal time to embark on your Cyclades adventure is a pivotal decision that can significantly shape your travel experience. Each season in the Cyclades offers a unique blend of weather conditions, cultural events, and crowd levels, allowing you to tailor your visit to match your preferences and desires. In this section, we will delve into the four distinct seasons that characterize the Cyclades archipelago, providing you with detailed insights to aid in making an informed decision about when to set sail.

### Springtime Bliss: Weather, Events, and Blossoming Landscapes

As the Cyclades awaken from their winter slumber, spring arrives with a burst of vibrant energy. The months from March to May bring mild temperatures and the islands come alive with a kaleidoscope of colorful blossoms. The rejuvenating atmosphere makes spring an appealing time to explore the Cyclades, particularly for those who prefer pleasant weather without the intense summer heat.

**Weather and Climate**: During spring, the Cyclades experience temperatures ranging from 15°C to 20°C (59°F to 68°F), creating comfortable conditions for outdoor exploration. Crisp mornings gradually give way to pleasantly warm afternoons, ideal for both sightseeing and beach activities.

**Blossoming Landscapes:** The islands transform into a floral paradise as wildflowers carpet the hillsides and olive groves. This season presents fantastic opportunities for nature lovers, photographers, and hikers to capture the Cyclades in full bloom.

**Cultural Events:** Spring marks the beginning of the festive season, with numerous cultural events celebrating local traditions and art. Easter, in particular, is a significant occasion, celebrated with elaborate processions, feasts, and religious ceremonies.

## Summer Sizzle: Embracing the Sun, Beaches, and Festivals

The summer months of June to August bring the quintessential Cycladic experience, characterized by sun-soaked days, crystalline waters, and a lively atmosphere. This is the peak tourist season, attracting travelers from around the world who come to bask in the islands' beauty and revel in their vibrant energy.

**Weather and Climate:** Summer is synonymous with sunshine, with temperatures ranging from 25°C to 30°C (77°F to 86°F). The clear skies and warm waters create ideal conditions for beach outings, water sports, and sunbathing.

**Beaches and Seaside Delights:** With the Mediterranean Sea at its warmest, summer is the best time to enjoy the

Cyclades' renowned beaches. Whether you're seeking vibrant beach clubs or secluded coves, the islands offer a diverse array of coastal experiences.

**Festivals and Nightlife:** Summer is a season of celebration in the Cyclades. Festivals, music events, and open-air concerts fill the evenings with excitement. The nightlife comes alive with beach parties, bars, and tavernas that stay open late into the night.

## Autumn Serenity: Mild Weather and Quieter Island Ambiance

September to November ushers in the serene charm of autumn in the Cyclades. As the summer crowds disperse, a sense of tranquility settles over the islands. This season offers a more relaxed pace of exploration, with pleasant weather and a variety of cultural experiences.

**Weather and Climate:** Autumn brings milder temperatures, ranging from 20°C to 25°C (68°F to 77°F), creating comfortable conditions for sightseeing and outdoor activities. The sea retains its warmth, allowing for enjoyable swimming and water-based pursuits.

**Cultural Experiences:** Autumn is a fantastic time to immerse yourself in the local way of life. Participate in wine harvest festivals, traditional feasts, and cultural events that showcase the islands' heritage.

## Winter Retreat: Exploring the Cyclades' Off-Peak Charms

From December to February, the Cyclades transition into their quietest season, providing an alternative perspective of the islands' beauty. While some activities and businesses may be limited during this period, winter offers a unique opportunity for travelers seeking solitude and an authentic local experience.

**Weather and Climate:** Winters in the Cyclades are mild, with temperatures ranging from 10°C to 15°C (50°F to 59°F). While the weather may be cooler, the islands' charm endures, and the absence of crowds allows for intimate exploration.

**Local Life and Culture:** Winter invites you to engage with the local community and embrace the unhurried pace of island life. Visit traditional tavernas, engage in conversations with locals, and experience the Cyclades in their most authentic form.

In conclusion, choosing the right time to explore the Cyclades involves understanding the unique characteristics of each season. Whether you seek the invigorating beauty of spring, the vibrant energy of summer, the serene ambiance of autumn, or the quiet charm of winter, each season offers a distinct perspective of these enchanting islands. Your preferences for weather, events, and crowd levels will determine the best time for your Cyclades adventure, ensuring a personalized and unforgettable experience in this Aegean paradise.

# Visa and Entry Requirements: Essential Travel Logistics

When embarking on your thrilling adventure to the Cyclades, it's essential to arm yourself with knowledge about the visa and entry requirements, particularly if you're a traveler hailing from outside the European Union (EU). Navigating these crucial travel logistics will set the tone for a seamless and stress-free start to your Cycladic exploration. This section is designed to equip you with a comprehensive understanding of the intricacies surrounding visas, entry regulations, and processes, ensuring that you're well-prepared for your journey.

**Visa Exemptions and Visa-On-Arrival Information**

For certain nationalities, Greece offers the convenience of visa exemptions or visa-on-arrival options, allowing you to enter the country without obtaining a visa in advance. The duration of stay and specific entry conditions may vary based on your nationality. Commonly, these exemptions and on-arrival provisions are limited to shorter visits, typically for tourism or business purposes. It's crucial to research and confirm the details pertaining to your own nationality to ensure you're in compliance with these regulations.

**Schengen Zone and Visa-Free Travel**

Greece, being a part of the Schengen Zone, operates under a unified visa policy alongside other EU member states. This policy enables travelers to move freely within the Schengen Area, which encompasses most of the European Union countries, without the need for internal border checks. If you possess a valid Schengen visa, issued by any of the Schengen member countries, you can explore the Cyclades and the broader region with ease. This is particularly advantageous if you plan to visit multiple destinations during your European journey.

**Entry Requirements for Non-EU Visitors**

If you're not a citizen of an EU member state or a country benefiting from visa exemptions, understanding the entry requirements is paramount. The process typically involves applying for a Schengen visa, specifically a Greece Schengen visa if your primary destination is within Greece, which covers your Cycladic adventure. This visa grants you access to the Cyclades and other Schengen states for the duration of your stay.

To initiate this process, you'll need to contact the Greek consulate or embassy in your home country. The application generally requires:

- Application Form: Complete and duly signed Schengen visa application form.
- Passport: A valid passport with a minimum of two blank pages and a validity extending beyond your intended departure date.
- Passport-Sized Photos: Provide recent passport-sized photographs adhering to the specified dimensions.

- Flight Itinerary: Present a confirmed round-trip flight itinerary indicating your entry and exit points.
- Accommodation Details: Confirmation of your accommodations within the Cyclades, demonstrating your planned stay.
- Travel Insurance: Comprehensive travel insurance coverage for medical expenses and repatriation throughout your trip.
- Proof of Financial Means: Evidence of sufficient funds to cover your stay, ensuring you won't become a financial burden during your time in Greece.
- Travel Itinerary: A detailed outline of your travel plans, including your intended Cyclades island-hopping route and any other destinations.

Keep in mind that the processing time for your Schengen visa application can vary based on your nationality and the volume of applications received by the consulate. Thus, it's advisable to apply well in advance of your intended travel dates to avoid any last-minute complications.

## Budgeting for the Trip: Accommodation, Transportation, and Daily Expenses

Budgeting is not just a practical necessity; it's a strategic tool that can enhance your travel experience. By understanding the expected costs of your Cyclades adventure, you'll be empowered to make informed decisions that align with your financial goals and preferences. This section dives into the financial aspects of your journey, ensuring that you can fully relish the beauty and culture of the Cycladic islands without any financial worries.

## Accommodation Options: Hotels, Villas, Hostels, and Guesthouses

When it comes to accommodations in the Cyclades, diversity is the name of the game. Whether you're a luxury seeker, a budget-conscious traveler, or somewhere in between, the islands offer a wide array of options to suit every taste and preference. As you plan your Cyclades adventure, consider the following accommodation choices to find your ideal home away from home.

### Hotels: Embracing Elegance and Views of the Aegean

Imagine waking up to the gentle sounds of the Aegean Sea and gazing out at the azure waters from your window. Upscale hotels in the Cyclades provide exactly this experience and more. With their prime locations and stunning views, these establishments offer a touch of luxury that harmonizes with the natural beauty of the islands. From Santorini's caldera-facing suites to Mykonos' boutique beachfront escapes, each island boasts its unique assortment of high-end hotels. Prices for these accommodations can vary significantly based on the island's popularity, the room's view, and the services provided. When selecting a hotel, it's essential to research thoroughly to ensure that you're getting the best value for your budget.

## *Villas: Crafting Personal Retreats in Paradise*

For those seeking a more private and spacious experience, renting a villa is an excellent choice. Villas offer an unparalleled sense of autonomy and comfort, making them ideal for families, groups, or travelers who relish their personal space. Many villas come equipped with kitchens, enabling you to prepare meals and reduce dining expenses. This option not only offers a homey atmosphere but also presents opportunities to immerse yourself in local life. Whether you're nestled amidst Naxos' vineyards or enjoying the tranquility of a Paros village, renting a villa adds an extra layer of authenticity to your Cyclades adventure.

## *Hostels and Guesthouses: Connecting with Travelers and Budgeting Wisely*

Budget-conscious travelers will find a haven in the Cyclades through hostels and guesthouses. These accommodations provide comfortable lodging without breaking the bank, freeing up your budget for island exploration and activities. Hostels often have dormitory-style rooms that encourage interactions with fellow travelers, making them perfect for solo adventurers or those seeking to forge new friendships. Guesthouses, on the other hand, provide a more private and intimate experience while maintaining budget-friendliness. These options, scattered across the islands, offer a practical way to experience the Cyclades without compromising on comfort.

Whether you're yearning for the lavishness of an upscale hotel, the privacy of a villa retreat, or the camaraderie of a hostel, the Cyclades cater to all preferences and budgets. As you embark on your island-hopping journey, the accommodation you choose will become your base for exploration and rejuvenation. So take your time to research, align your choices with your desired experience, and make your stay in the Cyclades an unforgettable chapter of your travel story.

## Transportation Costs: Ferry Tickets, Local Transport, and Car Rentals

The Cyclades' allure lies in their scattered beauty across the Aegean Sea, but reaching and traversing these islands comes with transportation costs that require strategic consideration. From the essential ferry tickets that link these gems to local transport options and potential car rentals, mastering this aspect of your budget is key to a smooth and enjoyable Cyclades adventure.

### Ferry Tickets: Seamlessly Island-Hopping the Cyclades

Ferry travel is the lifeblood of Cycladic exploration, connecting each island like beads on a necklace. To budget wisely, it's essential to understand the intricacies of ferry costs:

Variability in Prices: Ferry ticket costs are influenced by factors like the distance between islands, the type of ferry (standard, high-speed, or luxury), and the class of service (economy, business, etc.).

Booking in Advance: Booking your ferry tickets in advance can significantly reduce costs, as last-minute tickets tend to be more expensive, especially during peak seasons.

Multi-Island Passes: Some ferry companies offer multi-island passes that allow you to travel between several Cycladic islands at a discounted rate. These passes can be a cost-effective solution if your itinerary includes multiple stops.

**Local Transport: Island Mobility on a Budget**

Once you've disembarked on an island, efficient local transport becomes crucial for exploration. Here's what to consider:

Buses: Public buses are a cost-effective way to get around larger islands. They provide access to popular tourist areas and often have schedules aligned with ferry arrivals and departures.

Taxis: Taxis are convenient for door-to-door service, but they tend to be pricier compared to other options. Consider sharing rides or using taxis for shorter distances to save on costs.

Alternative Options: For shorter distances, walking is not only budget-friendly but also allows you to soak in the local ambiance. Renting a scooter or bicycle can also be a fun and affordable way to explore the island at your own pace.

## Car Rentals: A Balance of Convenience and Expense

Renting a car offers flexibility and convenience, especially if you want to explore the nooks and crannies of an island. However, before opting for this option, weigh the pros and cons:

Rental Fees: Car rental costs vary based on the type of vehicle, the rental duration, and the island. Smaller cars are generally more economical.

Fuel Costs: Factor in fuel expenses, which can add up if you're planning extensive exploration.

Parking Fees: Some islands have limited parking space, and parking fees might apply. Consider this when budgeting for a car rental.

Assessing Need: If your island-hopping adventure involves only a few stops, using local transport might be more cost-effective. Reserve car rentals for islands where you plan to explore extensively.

By delving into the intricacies of transportation costs in the Cyclades, you're not only setting the stage for a smoother journey but also unlocking the freedom to make choices that align with your budget and preferences. Whether you opt for ferry hopping, use local transport, or indulge in the convenience of a rental car, understanding these aspects allows you to allocate your funds wisely and enhance your overall Cyclades experience.

## Gauging Daily Expenses: Meals, Activities, and Souvenirs

In the enchanting realm of the Cycladic islands, daily expenses are your canvas to paint your unforgettable adventure. This canvas is composed of the vivid strokes of meals that tantalize your taste buds, the vibrant colors of activities that spark joy, and the intricate details of souvenirs that etch lasting memories. Mastering the art of budgeting these components ensures that your Cyclades journey is as fulfilling for your senses as it is for your soul.

### Meals: Savoring Cycladic Flavors

Dining in the Cyclades is an exploration of flavors, a symphony of culinary traditions spanning from humble street food to gourmet dining. Local tavernas, with their inviting ambiance, often provide a window into authentic island cuisine at reasonable prices. Here, you can enjoy delectable dishes that showcase the freshest catches from the Aegean and locally grown produce.

Local Tavernas: A cornerstone of Cycladic dining, these charming eateries offer hearty meals infused with tradition. Delight in dishes like moussaka, souvlaki, and fresh seafood without straining your budget.

Casual Cafés: For a lighter experience, cafés present an array of sandwiches, salads, and pastries. These options are not only budget-friendly but also perfect for a quick bite between activities.

Fine Dining Experiences: While a bit more lavish, fine dining establishments deliver a refined gastronomic encounter. Reserve these for special occasions, allowing yourself a taste of elevated Cycladic cuisine.

**Activities: Crafting Your Island Adventure**

Engaging in activities is where the essence of the Cyclades comes alive. Whether you're drawn to the crystal-clear waters, the ancient ruins, or the local traditions, each experience is a brushstroke on your travel canvas.

Water Sports: The Aegean's inviting waters beckon with opportunities for snorkeling, scuba diving, and kayaking. Prices can vary, so research and book water adventures that align with your budget and interests.

Guided Tours: Guided tours unravel the islands' history and hidden treasures. From exploring ancient ruins to strolling through charming villages, these tours offer rich insights. Prioritize the ones that captivate your curiosity while remaining within your allocated funds.

Cultural Experiences: Immerse yourself in the Cycladic culture through workshops, cooking classes, and local festivals. These interactive encounters provide a unique understanding of island life and are often budget-friendly.

**Souvenirs: Treasured Reminders of Your Journey**

Souvenirs are more than trinkets; they encapsulate the spirit of your travels. In the Cyclades, they range from handcrafted ceramics to intricate jewelry, capturing the islands' essence in tangible form.

Local Markets: Explore local markets and artisan stalls to find authentic souvenirs that support the island's craftsmen. Handwoven textiles, pottery, and intricate woodwork are just a few examples of the treasures you can discover.

Mindful Selection: While the desire to bring back mementos is strong, consider the significance of each item. Choose souvenirs that resonate with you and contribute to your journey's story, ensuring they align with your budget.

As you journey through the Cyclades, remember that your daily expenses are your toolkit for creating lasting memories. By savoring Cycladic flavors in a mix of dining experiences, engaging in activities that resonate with your passions, and thoughtfully selecting souvenirs that embody the islands' soul, you're crafting an authentic and enriching experience. Budgeting wisely for these components ensures that you can embrace the Cyclades' offerings while maintaining a harmonious balance between exploration and financial comfort. Your mastery of these financial details will allow you to roam the Cycladic islands with open-hearted enthusiasm, confident that each encounter and moment aligns perfectly with your vision of this unforgettable adventure.

# Chapter 2: Embarking on the Cycladic Odyssey

The journey to the Cyclades begins with your arrival in Athens, the vibrant capital of Greece. This chapter focuses on the essential aspects of your arrival, preparations, and how to set sail to embark on your island-hopping adventure.

## Athens as Your Gateway: Arrival and Preparations

### Arriving in Athens:

As you touch down in Athens, you're greeted by a city that seamlessly weaves together the threads of its rich history with the pulse of modern life. Whether you arrive by air or land, your entry into Athens marks the beginning of a remarkable journey through time and culture.

### *A City of Legends and Legacies:*

As you disembark from your flight or journey by train or bus, you'll immediately sense that Athens is a place where the past and present coexist in a captivating symphony. The city itself is steeped in myth and history, with its roots dating back thousands of years to the time of ancient Greece. The birthplace of democracy, philosophy, and theater, Athens exudes an aura of significance that is palpable from the moment you arrive.

### Ancient Treasures and Modern Marvels:

Athens boasts an array of architectural marvels that stand as living testaments to its glorious past. The iconic Acropolis, crowned by the Parthenon, dominates the city's skyline, an enduring reminder of the civilization that laid the foundations for Western culture. As you catch glimpses of this ancient citadel from various vantage points around the city, its majesty is sure to leave you in awe.

Yet, alongside these archaeological wonders, Athens is a city that's very much alive and pulsating with energy. Skyscrapers and contemporary buildings rise alongside historic structures, creating a dynamic juxtaposition that reflects the city's ongoing evolution. This blend of old and new can be seen in neighborhoods like Plaka, where narrow streets wind through charming alleys lined with traditional tavernas, artisan shops, and vibrant street art.

### Immersing in the Urban Beat:

Whether you're stepping out of Athens International Airport, known as Eleftherios Venizelos, or arriving at Athens Railway Station, the city's welcoming atmosphere envelopes you. Taxis and public transportation are readily available to take you to your chosen accommodations, whether you're seeking a luxury hotel with views of the Acropolis or a cozy guesthouse tucked away in a quiet corner.

As you venture further into Athens, you'll discover a vibrant urban tapestry. Explore the Monastiraki Flea Market, where antique treasures and eclectic wares are displayed against the backdrop of ancient ruins. Stroll along Ermou Street, a bustling shopping district offering a mix of international brands and local boutiques. Indulge in the city's culinary delights at traditional tavernas or chic restaurants, where you can savor Greek cuisine that has been perfected over generations.

***A Welcome to Remember:***

Arriving in Athens is not just about reaching a destination; it's about immersing yourself in a narrative that spans centuries. The city's energy and vitality provide a fitting prelude to the islands that await you in the Cyclades. Whether you choose to explore Athens for a day or two before embarking on your island-hopping adventure, or you linger longer to unravel its layers, the experience will leave an indelible mark.

As you soak in the bustling cityscape, with its ancient history and modern energy intertwining, you're poised to embark on a journey of contrasts and harmonies, where the mysteries of the past merge with the excitement of the present.

## Accommodation in Athens:

When embarking on your journey to the Cycladic islands, Athens often serves as the initial stepping stone, offering a fascinating blend of ancient history, vibrant culture, and modern amenities. As you plan your stay in the Greek capital, the choices for accommodation are as diverse as the city itself, catering to a wide range of preferences and budgets. From luxurious hotels that exude opulence to cozy budget-friendly hostels that foster a sense of community, Athens has something for everyone.

### *Luxury Hotels: Unveiling Opulence and Comfort*

For travelers seeking the pinnacle of comfort and indulgence, Athens presents an array of luxury hotels that seamlessly combine world-class amenities with exquisite design and personalized service. These upscale establishments offer a sanctuary of relaxation amidst the urban bustle. Guests can expect spacious, well-appointed rooms with elegant furnishings, often accompanied by breathtaking views of the Acropolis or the city skyline. Lavish on-site spas, fitness centers, and gourmet restaurants ensure a seamless blend of leisure and indulgence.

### *Boutique Charm: Discovering Unique Retreats*

Boutique hotels are scattered across Athens, providing a distinctively intimate and personalized experience. These hidden gems often boast distinct architectural designs, reflecting the city's rich history. Each room is carefully curated to offer a unique ambiance, allowing guests to immerse themselves in an atmosphere that celebrates both the past and the present. The attentive staff is dedicated to creating a memorable stay, offering recommendations for off-the-beaten-path experiences and local eateries.

## Mid-Range Comfort: Balancing Quality and Affordability

Mid-range hotels in Athens offer a balance between quality and affordability, catering to travelers who desire comfort without breaking the bank. These establishments provide well-equipped rooms, modern amenities, and convenient locations. Many mid-range hotels are strategically situated near popular attractions and transportation hubs, making it easy for guests to explore the city's treasures at their own pace.

## Budget-Friendly Hostels: Building Connections

For the budget-conscious traveler, Athens offers a vibrant hostel scene that encourages camaraderie and cultural exchange. Hostels provide dormitory-style accommodations that allow guests to connect with fellow travelers from around the world. Common areas, communal kitchens, and organized events foster a sense of community, making it an ideal choice for solo adventurers and those looking to make new friends.

## Plaka Neighborhood: Proximity to Historical Sites

While selecting your accommodation, consider staying in the Plaka neighborhood, a charming and historic district nestled at the base of the Acropolis. Plaka's narrow cobblestone streets, neoclassical architecture, and traditional tavernas offer an authentic Athenian experience. Staying in Plaka places you within walking distance of iconic landmarks such as the Acropolis, the Ancient Agora, and the Temple of

Olympian Zeus. The convenience of being close to these historical sites enables you to explore the city's rich past without the hassle of long commutes.

When searching for and booking accommodation in Athens, several apps can make your process smoother and more convenient. Here are some popular ones:

- Booking.com: This app offers a wide range of accommodation options, from hotels and hostels to apartments and guesthouses. It provides user reviews, detailed property descriptions, and a map view to help you choose the perfect place. The app often includes special deals and discounts as well.

- Airbnb: Airbnb is known for its diverse selection of accommodations, including entire homes, private rooms, and shared spaces. You can find unique stays and connect with local hosts. The app provides detailed listings, photos, and reviews to help you make an informed decision.

- Hotels.com: Hotels.com allows you to book hotels, resorts, and other accommodations. The app provides user reviews, photos, and a loyalty program that offers a free night's stay after booking a certain number of nights.

- Expedia: Expedia offers a comprehensive platform for booking flights, hotels, and vacation packages. The app provides exclusive deals, member pricing, and the ability to bundle your bookings for additional savings.

- Agoda: Agoda specializes in Asia-Pacific travel but offers global accommodation options. The app often provides competitive rates and exclusive deals on a variety of accommodations.

- Hostelworld: If you're looking for budget-friendly options like hostels, this app is perfect. It focuses on hostel bookings and provides user-generated reviews, photos, and ratings to help you choose the best fit.

- TripAdvisor: TripAdvisor offers reviews, ratings, and photos for accommodations along with restaurants and attractions. It's a great app to get a holistic view of your destination and make well-informed decisions.

- Trivago: Trivago compares hotel prices from various booking sites, helping you find the best deal. It also provides user reviews and ratings to aid your decision-making process.

- Hopper: While Hopper is primarily known for its flight booking capabilities, it also offers hotel bookings. The app predicts when hotel prices are likely to be the lowest and provides insights on when to book.

- Kayak: Kayak is a comprehensive travel app that not only helps you find accommodation but also offers flight and car rental options. It allows you to compare prices from different booking sites.

When using these apps, make sure to read reviews, check for special deals, and consider factors such as location, amenities, and guest ratings before finalizing your booking. Keep in mind that availability and prices may vary, so it's a good idea to book in advance, especially during peak travel seasons.

When choosing accommodation in Athens, you're presented with a spectrum of options that cater to your individual preferences, whether it's the opulent comfort of luxury hotels, the intimate charm of boutique stays, the convenience of mid-range establishments, or the camaraderie of budget-friendly hostels. To maximize your experience, consider staying in the Plaka neighborhood, where you'll be immersed in the city's history and within reach of its iconic landmarks. As you make your choice, remember that your accommodation is not just a place to rest your head; it's a gateway to discovering the captivating tapestry of Athens, a city where the past and the present intertwine in a truly magical way.

## Navigating Local Transport: Buses, Taxis, and Rental Services

### Arrival at Port:
The excitement swells as the ferry gently glides into the port of your chosen Cycladic island. As you disembark onto the sun-soaked dock, you're greeted by a new world of beauty and adventure. The first moments at the port are crucial for

setting the tone of your island-hopping experience, and this section will guide you through the essential steps to make the most of your arrival.

**Embracing the Port Atmosphere:**

The port area is often a hub of activity, bustling with fellow travelers, locals, and the scent of the sea. As you step off the ferry, take a moment to absorb the vibrant atmosphere around you. The salty breeze, the echoes of seagulls, and the sight of colorful boats create an authentic Cycladic ambiance that you'll remember throughout your journey.

**Orientation and Port Layout:**

Before venturing further, take a few minutes to orient yourself with the port layout. Look for directional signs that guide you to various areas, such as baggage claim, transportation hubs, and exit points. Many ports are designed to facilitate easy access to transportation options and tourist services.

**Tourist Information Centers:**

One of your first stops should be the local tourist information center. These centers are invaluable resources for obtaining maps, brochures, and guidance about the island's attractions and services. Friendly staff members are usually fluent in English and are eager to assist you with any questions or concerns. Gather information about must-visit sites, upcoming events, and local customs to enhance your island experience.

**Local Transportation Options:**

A myriad of transportation choices await you at the port. Buses, taxis, and sometimes even rental car counters are often conveniently located nearby. If you've researched transportation options in advance, this is the time to confirm your plans and gather any additional information you might need. If you prefer spontaneity, use this opportunity to ask locals or tourist center staff for recommendations based on your interests and the island's layout.

**Available Amenities:**

From cafes and restaurants to restrooms and ATMs, the port area typically offers a range of amenities to cater to travelers' needs. If you've just arrived and haven't had a chance to sample local cuisine, consider grabbing a bite at a waterfront eatery to savor your first tastes of Cycladic flavors.

**Absorbing the Initial Impressions:**

As you explore the port surroundings, let your senses take in the sights, sounds, and scents unique to the Cyclades. Absorb the charm of the local architecture, which often features whitewashed buildings with vibrant accents, typical of the region. Let the aura of anticipation infuse your spirit as you embark on your exploration of this new island paradise.

Arriving at the port of your first Cycladic island is a significant moment in your adventure. This initial encounter shapes your perception of the island and sets the stage for your island-hopping journey. By familiarizing yourself with the port layout, utilizing tourist information centers, exploring transportation options, and enjoying available amenities, you'll seamlessly transition from sea to land, ready to uncover the treasures that each Cycladic gem has to offer.

**Local Buses:**
When it comes to exploring the Cycladic islands, local buses play a crucial role in facilitating efficient and affordable transportation for both locals and tourists. These bus networks connect various villages, towns, beaches, and attractions, providing visitors with a convenient way to navigate the islands' landscapes and experience their unique charm. In this section, we delve into the intricacies of navigating the local bus networks on each Cycladic island, highlighting their significance, routes, timetables, and the overall experience they offer.

*** The Importance of Local Buses: Connecting Island Gems***

Local buses are the lifeline of transportation on the Cycladic islands, offering an economical and eco-friendly mode of getting around. The islands, known for their stunning landscapes and scattered settlements, often have winding roads that connect secluded beaches, traditional villages, archaeological sites, and vibrant towns. Local buses serve as the essential link between these destinations, allowing visitors to access both popular attractions and hidden gems with ease.

## Understanding Bus Routes and Timetables: Enhancing Your Travel Plans

Each Cycladic island boasts a unique bus network tailored to its topography, local needs, and attractions. Familiarizing yourself with the bus routes and timetables is a valuable step in optimizing your travel plans. Typically, the main bus terminal or station, located in the capital or a major town, serves as the starting point for various routes. From there, buses fan out to different parts of the island.

Routes: Bus routes are designed to cover key areas of interest. They often connect major towns, ports, beaches, historical sites, and sometimes even hiking trailheads. For example, a route might take you from the port to a popular beach, then onward to a historic village or a scenic viewpoint.

Timetables: Bus timetables are generally available at bus terminals, tourist information centers, or online platforms. They provide information about departure times, stops along the route, and estimated travel durations. It's important to note that schedules can vary based on the day of the week and the season, so it's a good idea to check for updates or changes, especially during holidays or off-peak seasons.

## Practical Tips for Riding Local Buses: Making the Most of Your Experience

- Plan Ahead: Before embarking on your bus journey, review the available routes and timetables to align with your itinerary. This ensures you don't miss a bus or end up waiting for an extended period.

- Arrive Early: Arriving at the bus stop a bit ahead of the scheduled departure time is advisable, as buses may sometimes arrive a few minutes early.

- Tickets and Payment: Most buses allow passengers to purchase tickets directly from the driver upon boarding. Make sure to have the correct change or small denominations of local currency.

- Comfort and Etiquette: Buses vary in terms of comfort. Some have air conditioning, while others might be more basic. Be mindful of other passengers and keep conversations and noise levels at a respectful level.

- Scenic Rides: Many bus routes on the Cycladic islands offer breathtaking views of the landscapes. Secure a window seat to soak in the beauty as you travel.

*Embracing the Local Experience: Beyond Convenience*

Riding the local buses on the Cycladic islands is more than just a means of transportation; it's an opportunity to immerse yourself in the local way of life. The buses are often frequented by both tourists and locals, providing a chance to interact, observe daily life, and perhaps even strike up conversations that lead to recommendations for hidden gems and authentic experiences.

The local bus networks on the Cycladic islands are integral to your exploration of these captivating destinations.

Understanding the routes, timetables, and the unique experience they offer will enable you to make the most of your journey, creating memories as you traverse the picturesque landscapes, vibrant towns, and tranquil beaches that define the Cycladic experience.

# Taxis:

When it comes to navigating the picturesque landscapes of the Cyclades, taxis offer both convenience and flexibility, providing an essential mode of transportation for travelers seeking comfort and efficiency. Understanding the availability of taxis, how to flag them down or arrange for pick-up, as well as gaining insights into negotiating fares and ensuring a smooth ride, can greatly enhance your island-hopping experience.

### *Availability and Accessibility*

Taxis are a common sight on most Cycladic islands, offering an accessible means of getting around for both locals and visitors. As you disembark from your ferry or explore the port areas, you'll find taxi stands conveniently situated, particularly near transportation hubs, popular tourist spots, and bustling squares. These designated taxi stands serve as gathering points where taxis await passengers, making it easy to find a ride without much effort.

### *Flagging Down Taxis*

Flagging down a taxi in the Cyclades is a straightforward process. As you approach a taxi stand or spot a taxi cruising the streets, simply extend your arm to signal that you need a ride. Taxis are typically marked with a prominent taxi sign on top and are often brightly colored, making them easily recognizable. It's a good practice to make eye contact with the driver to ensure they see your signal.

### *Arranging Pick-Up*

If you're not near a taxi stand or you prefer the convenience of having a taxi pick you up at a specific location, arranging for pick-up is also a viable option. Most islands have taxi dispatch services that you can call to request a taxi to your desired location. You can find these phone numbers at tourist information centers, on island maps, or even ask your accommodation provider for assistance. This option is particularly useful if you're staying in a less central area or need transportation during off-peak hours.

### *Negotiating Fares and Transparency*

Understanding the fare structure and ensuring transparency in taxi fares is an important aspect of your journey. Unlike metered taxis in larger cities, taxi fares on many Cycladic islands are often fixed for common routes, such as airport transfers or trips between major towns. However, it's still advisable to confirm the fare with the driver before starting the journey. This helps avoid any misunderstandings and sets expectations clearly.

### *Tips for Negotiating Fares*

- Confirm the Fare: Before you enter the taxi, inquire about the fare for your destination. This not only ensures that you're aware of the cost but also establishes a transparent understanding with the driver.

- Multiple Passengers: If you're traveling with a group or carrying additional luggage, it's prudent to confirm whether there are any extra charges for these factors.

- Language Assistance: While many taxi drivers in popular tourist areas speak English, having your destination written down or saved on your phone can help in cases of language barriers.

- Exact Change: Carrying small denominations of local currency can be helpful for paying the exact fare.

## *Ensuring a Smooth Ride*

To make your taxi journey as smooth as possible, consider these additional tips:

- Seat Belts: Ensure you and your fellow passengers are buckled up for safety.
- Travel Time: While taxis provide convenience, traffic conditions and the time of day can impact travel time. Plan accordingly, especially if you have time-sensitive engagements.
- Local Insight: Taxi drivers often have a wealth of local knowledge and can provide recommendations for

hidden gems, local eateries, and lesser-known attractions.

By understanding the dynamics of taxis in the Cyclades – from flagging down a cab to negotiating fares and ensuring a seamless ride – you'll be better equipped to navigate these stunning islands with ease, adding yet another layer of excitement to your unforgettable island-hopping adventure.

## Car and Scooter Rentals:

One of the most exhilarating ways to experience the Cyclades is by renting a car or scooter, providing you with unparalleled freedom and flexibility to explore these beautiful islands at your own pace. This mode of transportation allows you to delve deep into hidden gems, access remote beaches, and uncover lesser-known villages that might be off the beaten path.

### Discovering the Joys of Island Exploration

Renting a car or scooter offers a liberating sense of adventure. As you drive along the winding coastal roads, you'll have the luxury of stopping wherever catches your eye, capturing breathtaking views and taking spontaneous detours. The Cyclades, known for their picturesque landscapes and charming villages, invite you to immerse yourself in their beauty on your own terms.

### Tailoring Your Itinerary

With a rental vehicle at your disposal, you're in control of your itinerary. Whether you're drawn to the iconic sights or yearning for hidden treasures, you can create a personalized journey that matches your preferences and interests. The Cyclades boast a diverse range of experiences, from historical sites and archaeological wonders to idyllic beaches and tranquil valleys. Having your own transportation allows you to craft a bespoke adventure that resonates with you.

## Insights into the Rental Process

Before embarking on your island-hopping journey, it's essential to understand the rental process. Most major islands in the Cyclades offer car and scooter rental services, typically located near popular tourist areas or ports. You'll need a valid driver's license and, depending on local regulations, an international driving permit. Keep in mind that some rental agencies might have age restrictions, so it's advisable to confirm these details in advance.

## Driving Regulations and Safety Considerations

Familiarize yourself with the local driving regulations to ensure a safe and enjoyable experience. Remember that in Greece, as in many other countries, you drive on the right-hand side of the road. Adhere to speed limits and traffic rules, which can vary from island to island. While the roads in popular tourist areas are well-maintained, some rural routes might be narrower or less developed, requiring extra caution.

## Parking and Navigation Tips

Parking spaces in densely populated areas can be limited, particularly during peak seasons. Many islands have designated parking zones, and some accommodations offer parking facilities. Keep in mind that parking near popular attractions or beaches might require a bit of strategic planning. Additionally, having a GPS device or a reliable navigation app can greatly assist in navigating the islands and finding your desired destinations.

*Environmental Considerations*

While renting a car or scooter provides convenience, it's also important to be mindful of the environment. The Cyclades are known for their stunning natural beauty, and responsible tourism practices help preserve the integrity of these landscapes. Stick to designated roads and paths, and avoid venturing off-road to protect delicate ecosystems.

Renting a car or scooter in the Cyclades offers a dynamic and immersive way to explore these enchanting islands. It empowers you to shape your journey, discover hidden corners, and connect with the Cycladic essence on a deeper level. As you navigate the diverse landscapes and embrace the freedom of the open road, you'll create memories that linger long after your journey through the Cyclades comes to an end.

# Cycling and Walking:

In the realm of the Cycladic islands, where time seems to slow down and the paradisiacal landscapes beckon exploration, the modes of transportation themselves become part of the adventure. While ferries and buses offer convenient mobility, the enchanting allure of some islands invites travelers to immerse themselves in the timeless beauty on two wheels or by foot. Cycling and walking emerge as cherished methods to intimately engage with the islands' treasures, blending leisure with discovery in a way that leaves an indelible mark on the traveler's heart.

## *The Cycladic Island Rhythm: Slow Travel in a Fast World*

Cycling and walking epitomize the art of "slow travel," a concept that embraces a mindful approach to exploration, savoring every step and pedal rotation along the way. In a world often caught in a whirlwind of fast-paced experiences, these modes of transportation offer a refreshing contrast. As you embark on a leisurely bike ride or a tranquil stroll through charming villages and serene landscapes, you connect with the islands' essence on a deeper level, embracing the unhurried rhythm that these enchanting locales inspire.

## *Cycling Adventures: Unveiling the Islands' Hidden Gems*

Bike rentals are readily available on several Cycladic islands, granting you the freedom to chart your course through quaint cobblestone streets, coastal pathways, and scenic countryside. As you pedal along, the gentle breeze whispers tales of the land's history and culture. Discover hidden coves that remain concealed from the main roads, stumble upon local markets brimming with artisan crafts, and uncover vantage points that offer panoramic views of the Aegean Sea's azure expanse.

One of the benefits of cycling is the opportunity to journey off the beaten path. Venture away from crowded tourist areas and uncover the authentic soul of the islands. Encounter locals tending to their fields, fishermen mending their nets, and traditional tavernas exuding the irresistible aromas of freshly prepared delicacies. Each pedal rotation invites serendipitous encounters and allows you to curate your own experiences, away from schedules and time constraints.

### *Strolling Through Time: Walking Tours and Tranquil Exploration*

On foot, the islands unfold like a living storybook. Many towns and villages are designed with pedestrians in mind, with narrow lanes that wind through whitewashed buildings adorned with vibrant bougainvillaea. Walking tours offer a blend of history and folklore as you traverse ancient ruins, ornate churches, and charming squares that capture the essence of each island's unique character.

Immersing yourself in the pace of walking allows for deeper introspection and a connection to the surroundings that is often missed in the hurried rush of modern travel. Each step becomes an opportunity to absorb the sights, sounds, and scents of the islands, from the rhythmic lapping of waves against the shore to the aromatic wafts of traditional bakeries.

## *Embracing Sustainability and Responsible Travel*

Cycling and walking not only immerse you in the islands' beauty but also align with the principles of sustainable and responsible travel. By opting for these eco-friendly modes of transportation, you minimize your carbon footprint and contribute to the preservation of the islands' delicate ecosystems. As you cycle along picturesque routes and meander through charming villages, you become a participant in the islands' ongoing story, leaving only footprints and memories behind.

In essence, cycling and walking in the Cyclades are not just means of getting from point A to point B; they're integral parts of the journey itself. They allow you to traverse the islands with a sense of intimacy, inviting you to savor the present moment and forge a deeper connection with the land, its people, and its timeless allure. So, whether you choose to pedal along coastal paths or stroll through historic streets, the Cycladic islands welcome you to explore at your own pace and create memories that will forever linger in your heart.

# Chapter 3: Exploring Cyclades' Jewels

## Santorini: A Caldera of Beauty and Romance

Santorini, often hailed as the jewel of the Cyclades, is a destination that transcends mere description. With its captivating sunsets, dramatic volcanic landscapes, and unique Cycladic architecture, Santorini presents a perfect blend of natural beauty and romantic allure. This chapter delves into the island's highlights, focusing on the enchanting towns of Fira and Oia, as well as the unforgettable experiences that await in its wineries and amidst its volcanic formations.

**Exploring Fira and Oia**

**Fira**: The capital of Santorini, Fira, is a bustling hub that offers a perfect blend of historical charm and modern amenities. Perched on the cliffside, the town boasts breathtaking panoramic views of the caldera, the submerged crater created by a massive volcanic eruption. Visitors can explore narrow winding streets lined with white-washed buildings adorned with blue domes and colorful bougainvillaeas. The town is teeming with boutique shops, art galleries, and inviting cafes where you can sip on traditional Greek coffee while overlooking the azure waters below.

**Oia**: Often referred to as the crown jewel of Santorini, Oia is renowned for its iconic blue-domed churches and unparalleled sunset vistas. This picturesque village is a haven for artists, photographers, and dreamers seeking a taste of Cycladic paradise. Oia's charm lies in its winding cobblestone streets that lead to awe-inspiring viewpoints, making it a prime spot for capturing the perfect sunset photo. While exploring Oia, don't miss the chance to visit the Maritime Museum, which provides insight into Santorini's seafaring history.

## Sunsets, Volcanic Landscapes, and Wineries

Sunsets: Santorini's sunsets are legendary, and they draw visitors from around the world to witness the sun dipping below the horizon, casting hues of orange, pink, and gold across the sky and sea. One of the best spots to experience this natural spectacle is from Oia's Castle, where you can watch the sun's descent over the caldera, creating an ethereal and romantic atmosphere.

Volcanic Landscapes: The island's volcanic origins are evident in its landscapes, particularly at sites like the caldera cliffs and the Red Beach. A must-do excursion is a boat trip to the islet of Nea Kameni, which sits within the caldera. Here, you can hike to the crater of the still-active volcano, taking in panoramic views of the surrounding islands and the sea. The therapeutic hot springs at Palea Kameni offer a unique experience, where you can soak in the mineral-rich waters formed by volcanic activity.

Wineries: Santorini's volcanic soil contributes to its unique terroir, making it a haven for wine enthusiasts. The island is famed for its indigenous grape varieties, particularly the Assyrtiko grape, known for producing crisp and aromatic white wines. Embark on a wine-tasting journey through some of Santorini's renowned wineries, such as Santo Wines and Venetsanos Winery. Many wineries offer tours that provide insights into the winemaking process, along with the opportunity to savor local wines while gazing out at the caldera's stunning views.

## Ancient Akrotiri: Unveiling Santorini's Buried Legacy

As you traverse the picturesque landscapes and marvel at the stunning sunsets of Santorini, it's easy to get lost in the island's romantic charm. Yet, beneath the idyllic surface lies a hidden treasure that offers a glimpse into the island's ancient past: the archaeological site of Akrotiri. Often referred to as the "Minoan Pompeii," this remarkable Bronze Age settlement provides an intriguing window into a sophisticated civilization that once flourished on the island.

Around 1600 BCE, a cataclysmic volcanic eruption rocked the island, burying the settlement of Akrotiri beneath layers of volcanic ash and pumice. This natural disaster, while devastating, unintentionally preserved the city in a state of exceptional preservation, much like its more famous counterpart, Pompeii. Rediscovered in the late 1960s, the site has since been meticulously excavated, revealing a wealth of insights into the daily life, culture, and advancements of the ancient inhabitants.

Visiting the Akrotiri archaeological site is akin to stepping back in time. The carefully excavated ruins of houses, streets, and even an advanced drainage system offer a remarkable view of the layout and infrastructure of the city. Intricately crafted pottery, frescoes, and artifacts give us a glimpse of the aesthetic sensibilities and artistic talents of its people. The "House of the Ladies," for instance, boasts exquisite frescoes depicting graceful figures and scenes of daily life.

The layout of the city suggests meticulous urban planning, with multi-story buildings and paved streets hinting at a well-organized and prosperous society. The advanced architectural techniques employed by the inhabitants demonstrate their engineering prowess, as evidenced by the system of indoor plumbing and intricate stone masonry.

One of the most captivating aspects of the Akrotiri site is the way it challenges preconceptions about ancient societies. The highly developed urban infrastructure, the intricacy of the frescoes, and the evidence of international trade all paint a picture of a civilization that was both advanced and interconnected with the broader world of its time.

## Caldera Cruises: Sailing the Romantic Waves

While Santorini's allure is undeniable from land, the perspective from the sea is equally captivating, if not more so. The island's unique volcanic geography is best appreciated by embarking on a caldera cruise, an experience that combines romance, exploration, and natural beauty into one unforgettable journey.

Picture yourself aboard a traditional Greek fishing boat or a luxurious catamaran, setting sail into the azure expanse of the Aegean Sea. As you glide through the waters, the iconic towns of Fira and Oia gradually recede, revealing their whitewashed facades clinging to the cliffs. The caldera's towering cliffs and rock formations, tinted with the volcanic history of the island, create a breathtaking backdrop.

The sea breeze rustles your hair as you find a comfortable spot on deck, perhaps lounging on a plush cushioned seat or perched on the boat's edge, legs dangling over the clear waters. As the boat drifts along, you'll have the chance to dive into the crystal-clear waters for a refreshing swim. The experience of swimming in the caldera's unique volcanic setting is nothing short of extraordinary – a memory that will remain etched in your mind.

As the sun begins its descent towards the horizon, the scene transforms into a spectacle of colors. The sky ignites with hues of orange, pink, and gold, casting a warm glow over the sea. This magical interplay of light and color sets the stage for a romantic sunset that seems to be painted just for you. Couples cuddle, friends share laughter, and families come together to witness nature's most enchanting display.

Culminating this dreamy voyage is the delectable Mediterranean meal prepared by the onboard crew. Whether you're savoring fresh seafood, local delicacies, or simply enjoying a glass of wine, the experience is a sensory delight that perfectly complements the visual feast of the setting sun. As the sun sinks beneath the horizon, casting a last blaze of color across the sky, you'll carry the memory of this unique journey in your heart forever.

## Artistic Inspirations: The Island's Muse

Beyond its physical beauty and historical significance, Santorini has long been an artistic muse, inspiring creators from all walks of life. The island's luminous colors, unique architecture, and timeless landscapes have the power to ignite the creative spark within any artist.

For painters, Santorini offers a vibrant palette of colors that seem to come alive under the Aegean sun. The contrast between the white-washed buildings and the deep blue sea, punctuated by the occasional dome or bougainvillaea, creates a picturesque scene begging to be captured on canvas. Artists often find themselves setting up easels in narrow streets or on quiet corners, trying to capture the essence of the island's beauty.

Writers, too, find inspiration in the island's rich tapestry of history and mythology. Santorini's past, interwoven with tales of ancient civilizations, volcanic eruptions, and cultural exchanges, provides ample material for storytelling. From the legend of Atlantis to the stories of Greek gods and heroes, the island's mystique lends itself to narratives that bridge the gap between the past and the present.

Photographers, in particular, find themselves in a paradise of visual wonder. Santorini's iconic blue domes, windmills, and dramatic cliffs make for postcard-perfect images that capture the essence of the Cyclades. Whether you're a professional photographer or simply someone with a smartphone, the vistas of Santorini present a never-ending opportunity to capture stunning moments that will forever remind you of the island's allure.

## Santorini's Underwater World: A Marine Wonderland

Beyond the charming streets and majestic cliffs of Santorini lies another world waiting to be explored – the island's underwater realm. For those who are captivated by marine life and the mysteries of the deep sea, Santorini offers an aquatic adventure that is as enchanting as its landscapes above the waterline.

Scuba diving and snorkeling excursions around Santorini reveal a hidden world of vibrant marine ecosystems. The crystal-clear waters offer excellent visibility, allowing you to witness the vibrant corals, rock formations, and a diverse array of marine creatures that call these waters home. Exploring the underwater caves, swim-throughs, and crevices adds an element of discovery to your island journey.

The underwater life around Santorini is a testament to the island's volcanic origins. The volcanic activity has created a unique underwater topography, with submerged craters, volcanic rocks, and underwater walls. These formations provide habitats for an array of marine species, from colorful fish to octopuses, eels, and even the occasional dolphin or sea turtle.

Whether you're a seasoned diver or a beginner looking to experience the thrill of breathing underwater, Santorini's dive sites cater to all skill levels. Professional dive centers offer guided excursions, ensuring safety and providing insights into the marine environment. As you descend into the depths, you'll be mesmerized by the vibrant colors, the sense of weightlessness, and the quiet beauty that characterizes Santorini's underwater world.

Santorini's underwater experiences extend beyond just diving and snorkeling. For those interested in a more immersive exploration, you can engage in underwater photography or even embark on a specialized course to learn more about marine life and conservation efforts.

In conclusion, Santorini's treasures extend far beyond its stunning sunsets and charming towns. From its ancient past at the Akrotiri archaeological site to the romantic escapades on caldera cruises, the island offers a myriad of experiences that cater to history enthusiasts, romantics, artists, and marine adventurers alike. The allure of Santorini is not confined to the surface – it seeps into the depths of its history, culture, and natural wonders, creating a destination that is as multifaceted as it is captivating.

As you explore Santorini's towns, bask in its sunsets, traverse its volcanic terrains, and savor its unique wines, you'll undoubtedly be enchanted by the island's aura of romance and wonder. Santorini's distinctive blend of natural beauty and cultural richness makes it a crown jewel within the Cyclades, offering an experience that lingers in the hearts of all who visit.

## Mykonos: The Glamorous Playground of the Cyclades

Nestled in the heart of the Cyclades archipelago, Mykonos stands as a beacon of luxury, beauty, and vibrant energy. Often referred to as the "Island of the Winds," Mykonos offers a captivating blend of traditional Cycladic charm and contemporary glamour. From the captivating streets of Chora to the iconic windmills that adorn its landscape, and from the renowned beach clubs to the exhilarating nightlife, Mykonos is a destination that promises an unforgettable experience.

### Chora's Charm and Iconic Windmills

The beating heart of Mykonos is undoubtedly Chora, the island's main town. As you wander through its labyrinthine streets, you'll find yourself immersed in a world of whitewashed buildings adorned with colorful doors and windows. The distinct architecture of Mykonos reflects both its Cycladic heritage and its history as a maritime hub. The narrow streets, often too narrow for cars, are designed to provide shade and protection from the strong winds that sweep through the island.

A stroll through Chora will lead you to the iconic windmills that have become the symbol of Mykonos. Perched on a hill overlooking the town and the azure Aegean Sea, these windmills were once vital to the island's economy, serving as grain mills during the 16th century. Today, they stand as a picturesque reminder of Mykonos' past, offering visitors breathtaking panoramic views and the perfect backdrop for memorable photographs.

## Beach Clubs, Nightlife, and Beyond

Mykonos is renowned for its pristine beaches, and what better way to experience them than through its exclusive beach clubs? The island boasts a collection of world-class beach establishments that cater to those seeking relaxation, entertainment, and a touch of glamour. Psarou Beach, for instance, is home to Nammos, a lavish beach club frequented by celebrities and travelers alike. Here, you can indulge in luxury lounging, fine dining, and a vibrant social scene.

As the sun sets over the Aegean, Mykonos transforms into a playground of nightlife and entertainment. The island is famous for its vibrant party scene, drawing visitors from around the world to its energetic bars, clubs, and lounges. The district of Little Venice, named for its proximity to the sea and its quaint houses that seem to float on the water's edge, is a prime spot to start your evening. With its charming ambience and seafront restaurants, it's the perfect place to enjoy a cocktail while watching the sun dip below the horizon.

The nightlife in Mykonos is eclectic and caters to a diverse crowd. Whether you're seeking a laid-back beachside bar or a high-energy dance club, you'll find options to suit your preferences. Clubs like Cavo Paradiso and Paradise Club are renowned for hosting world-famous DJs and throwing unforgettable parties that last well into the early hours of the morning.

But Mykonos offers more than just beaches and nightlife. The island's cultural richness can be explored through its museums, galleries, and historical sites. The Archaeological Museum of Mykonos, for instance, houses a collection of artifacts that showcase the island's ancient past. From prehistoric pottery to sculptures and jewelry, these treasures provide insight into the island's significance throughout history.

## Luxury Shopping and Designer Boutiques: Mykonos' Fashion Haven

Mykonos, often celebrated for its stunning beaches and vibrant nightlife, offers an unexpected delight for the fashion connoisseur. The island has transformed into a paradise for those with a penchant for luxury shopping and designer boutiques. Wandering through the picturesque streets of Mykonos, visitors are greeted by an array of upscale stores, featuring a blend of renowned international designers and local artisans. This unique shopping experience is set against the backdrop of the island's iconic Cycladic architecture, creating a harmonious fusion of style and tradition.

Strolling along the narrow lanes of Chora, Mykonos' main town, shoppers are captivated by an array of high-end fashion boutiques that showcase the latest trends and exclusive collections. From the elegant creations of world-renowned fashion houses to the handcrafted designs of local artisans, Mykonos offers a range of options to satiate every fashion desire.

Jewelry enthusiasts are in for a treat, as Mykonos boasts a selection of exquisite jewelry boutiques that showcase intricate pieces inspired by the island's beauty and culture. From intricate gold designs to precious gemstones, these jewelry boutiques offer the perfect blend of luxury and authenticity.

What sets Mykonos apart is its ability to cater to diverse tastes while maintaining a sense of exclusivity. The island's shopping experience extends beyond clothing and accessories, encompassing a plethora of unique souvenirs and home décor items. Handcrafted ceramics, traditional textiles, and intricate artworks provide travelers with the opportunity to take home a piece of Mykonos' distinctive charm.

## Delve into History: Delos Island Excursion

For history enthusiasts and curious explorers, a short boat ride from Mykonos leads to the awe-inspiring Delos Island. This UNESCO World Heritage Site is steeped in mythology and history, believed to be the birthplace of the Greek deities Apollo and Artemis. The significance of Delos extends beyond its mythological associations; the island once served as a bustling religious and commercial center in ancient times.

Stepping onto the shores of Delos, visitors are greeted by the ruins of ancient temples, marketplaces, and grand residences. The Terrace of the Lions, a row of iconic marble lion statues, stands as a sentinel of the island's rich past. The Archaeological Museum of Delos further enriches the experience, displaying artifacts unearthed from the island's excavations, including intricate sculptures, mosaics, and pottery.

Exploring Delos is like stepping back in time, as the well-preserved ruins offer insights into the daily lives and beliefs of ancient inhabitants. The Sacred Lake, the Temple of Isis, and the House of Dionysus are just a few of the captivating sites that provide a window into the island's historical significance.

## Art and Galleries: Mykonos' Creative Pulse

Beyond its reputation as a party hotspot, Mykonos also nurtures a vibrant art scene that adds an extra layer of cultural depth to its glamorous ambiance. The island's creative pulse is evident through its numerous art galleries that showcase an eclectic range of works by local and international artists.

Visitors can explore contemporary art pieces that challenge conventions, as well as traditional crafts that pay homage to Cycladic heritage. The galleries are carefully curated to provide a diverse and captivating selection of paintings, sculptures, and mixed-media creations. From abstract interpretations to vivid depictions of island landscapes, Mykonos' art galleries are a testament to the island's ability to inspire and captivate.

The art scene isn't confined to traditional gallery spaces; public art installations and street art contribute to the island's dynamic creative atmosphere. As you stroll through the streets, you may stumble upon vibrant murals and thought-provoking sculptures that add a touch of artistic flair to Mykonos' charm.

## Celebrity Hotspot and Paparazzi Haven

Mykonos has earned its status as a celebrity hotspot, attracting A-listers from around the world who are drawn to the island's allure and exclusivity. The blend of luxury accommodations, high-end dining, and captivating ambiance makes Mykonos a favorite destination for those seeking both privacy and a taste of the glamorous lifestyle.

The island's exclusive beach clubs and upscale resorts provide the ideal backdrop for relaxation and indulgence.

Visitors can unwind on pristine beaches while sipping cocktails, surrounded by unparalleled beauty. The seamless fusion of natural splendor and opulent comfort contributes to Mykonos' status as a haven for the rich and famous.

It's important to note that Mykonos has cultivated a paparazzi-friendly environment, further amplifying its allure. The presence of celebrities and their social media posts showcasing the island's beauty have contributed to Mykonos' reputation as a destination that encapsulates luxury, style, and the allure of fame.

## Wellness and Relaxation Retreats: Finding Serenity Amidst Glamour

Beyond the glitz and glamour, Mykonos also offers a serene retreat for those seeking wellness and rejuvenation. The island's tranquil Cycladic landscapes provide the perfect backdrop for relaxation, and a range of luxury spas, yoga retreats, and wellness centers cater to visitors' desires for holistic well-being.

Mykonos' wellness offerings encompass a diverse range of experiences, from soothing spa treatments that utilize natural ingredients to invigorating yoga sessions by the sea. Visitors can immerse themselves in meditation, indulge in massages, and practice yoga in serene settings that foster inner peace and self-discovery.

The wellness retreats on Mykonos are carefully designed to align with the island's enchanting energy, providing a harmonious blend of glamour and serenity. Whether seeking to unwind after a night of revelry or simply to escape the pressures of daily life, Mykonos' wellness offerings provide a pathway to restoration amidst its captivating beauty.

In conclusion, Mykonos is a destination that effortlessly balances tradition with modernity, tranquility with excitement, and natural beauty with luxurious indulgence. Its picturesque Chora, iconic windmills, opulent beach clubs, and bustling nightlife make it a glamorous playground for travelers seeking an unparalleled experience in the Cyclades. Whether you're looking to relax on pristine beaches, dance the night away, or immerse yourself in the island's rich history, Mykonos promises an enchanting journey that will leave an indelible mark on your travel memories.

# Naxos: Where Tradition Meets Tranquility

Nestled within the heart of the Cyclades archipelago, Naxos stands as a captivating testament to the intersection of tradition and tranquility. This island, with its rich history and diverse landscapes, offers a unique blend of cultural exploration and serene beauty that enchants every traveler fortunate enough to visit. From the bustling Naxos Town to the heights of Mount Zeus, and the immersive cultural experiences in between, Naxos promises an unforgettable journey.

# Naxos Town and Portara: Where the Past Meets Present

As the gateway to Naxos, Naxos Town (also known as Chora) welcomes visitors with an enchanting blend of narrow alleys, vibrant squares, and Venetian architecture. The imposing Portara, a massive marble doorway, stands as a sentinel on the islet of Palatia, just off the coast of Naxos Town. This ancient monument is the sole remnant of an unfinished temple dedicated to Apollo, and its silhouette against the Aegean sunset offers a sight that's equally poetic and profound.

The walk to Portara is a leisurely journey that provides insights into the island's history and charm. Strolling along the waterfront promenade, you'll find cozy cafes and quaint shops, perfect for a midday break. The Archaeological Museum of Naxos, housed in a Venetian mansion, showcases a collection of artifacts that narrate the island's historical tapestry.

As the sun begins to set, embark on the short but rewarding hike to Portara. The golden hues of the sinking sun cast a warm glow over the monument, creating an ambiance that's both contemplative and romantic. The views of Naxos Town and the surrounding coastline are awe-inspiring, making Portara a photographer's paradise and a place to witness the marriage of history and natural beauty.

# Hiking Mount Zeus and Cultural Immersion

For those seeking a more active exploration, Naxos offers the opportunity to hike Mount Zeus, the highest peak in the Cyclades. This invigorating journey takes you through a landscape adorned with wildflowers, fragrant herbs, and panoramic vistas that stretch across the Aegean Sea. The trail weaves its way through traditional villages, offering a glimpse into the island's rural lifestyle.

As you ascend, the vistas become increasingly breathtaking, revealing the patchwork of Naxos' countryside and the surrounding islands. The sense of accomplishment upon reaching the summit is immeasurable. Mount Zeus rewards hikers with a sweeping panorama that captures the essence of Naxos—a harmonious blend of azure waters, rolling hills, and charming settlements.

Beyond its natural beauty, Naxos invites you to immerse yourself in its cultural fabric. The island's history is entwined with its agriculture, and you can partake in workshops that celebrate age-old traditions. Engage in the art of cheese-making, as Naxos is renowned for its production of fine cheeses, particularly the beloved graviera. Learn about local farming practices and the cultivation of citron, a fragrant citrus fruit unique to the island.

Exploring the villages of Naxos, such as Apeiranthos with its labyrinthine streets and marble-paved squares, provides a glimpse into the island's past. The Folklore Museum of

Apeiranthos provides insights into the island's rural life, with exhibits that showcase traditional costumes, tools, and crafts.

## Delos Excursions: Exploring Ancient History

Mykonos, with its sun-soaked beaches and vibrant nightlife, is often associated with modern-day indulgence. Yet, just a short boat trip away lies a treasure trove of ancient history that beckons to be explored: the island of Delos. This UNESCO World Heritage Site stands as a testament to a bygone era, a place where the ruins of temples, houses, and marketplaces whisper stories of a once-thriving religious and cultural center.

Setting sail from Mykonos, the journey to Delos is both a physical and mental transition. As the boat glides across the azure waters of the Aegean, you can almost feel the centuries fall away, immersing yourself in the footsteps of ancient travelers who sought spiritual enlightenment and artistic inspiration on this sacred island.

Upon arrival, the ruins unfold like a tapestry of history, woven over centuries of human activity. The Avenue of the Lions welcomes you with its imposing marble statues, guardians of an era long past. You'll wander through the remnants of grand temples, including the Temple of Apollo, which stood as the heart of Delos' religious life. The Terrace of the Lions, another iconic feature, stands as a haunting reminder of the island's significance in the ancient world.

Exploring the well-preserved mosaic floors, the remnants of intricate frescoes, and the once-bustling agora, you'll get a glimpse into daily life on this hallowed ground. The House of Dionysus and the House of Cleopatra reveal the lavish lifestyles of the island's elite, while the amphitheater echoes with the distant applause of long-forgotten performances.

As you walk amidst the ruins, it's as if the past comes alive, whispering secrets of Delos' former glory. The sense of awe that envelops you is not solely due to the archaeological significance, but also the spiritual weight of the place. Delos was believed to be the birthplace of Apollo and Artemis, the twin deities that played pivotal roles in Greek mythology. This connection to the divine infuses the island with an aura that's both reverent and humbling.

The interplay between the historical remnants and the breathtaking natural surroundings is equally captivating. The island's landscapes, from rugged cliffs to serene beaches, create a backdrop that enhances the ethereal quality of Delos. Taking a moment to stand amidst the ruins and gaze across the sea, you can almost envision the ships of ancient mariners approaching the island, guided by Apollo's light.

As you bid farewell to Delos and return to Mykonos, you carry with you not just the memories of a captivating journey, but a deeper understanding of the intricate web that connects the past, the present, and the human spirit. The exploration of Delos transcends the boundaries of time, offering a chance to touch the threads of history and to stand in awe of the remarkable achievements of those who came before us.

## Windmills and Little Venice: Iconic Landmarks

While Mykonos has earned its reputation as a glamorous haven for beachgoers and party enthusiasts, the island's allure extends beyond its lively shores. As the sun sets over the Aegean Sea, a new facet of Mykonos emerges—one that's adorned with iconic landmarks that have etched themselves into the hearts of travelers.

Perched gracefully on a hill overlooking Mykonos Town, the iconic windmills of Mykonos stand as both a symbol of the island's heritage and a testament to its enduring charm. These iconic structures, with their stark white walls and conical roofs, present a scene that's as picturesque as it is timeless. Historically used for milling wheat, these windmills evoke a sense of nostalgia and provide a window into Mykonos' agricultural past.

The windmills' strategic location allows them to catch the brisk Aegean breeze, their wooden sails turning rhythmically in a dance that's been choreographed by the elements for generations. As the sun dips below the horizon, the windmills become silhouettes against the golden sky, creating an image that's both serene and mesmerizing. This vantage point is favored by photographers, capturing a blend of nature and culture that defines Mykonos' essence.

Descending from the windmills, the enchanting district of Little Venice beckons with its colorful houses that appear to emerge directly from the sea. This charming neighborhood exudes an atmosphere of romanticism and poetic nostalgia. Balconies adorned with bougainvillaeas spill over turquoise waters, and the sounds of lapping waves harmonize with the soft melodies drifting from the nearby tavernas.

Little Venice's allure is magnified during the magical hours of sunset. As the sun paints the sky with hues of orange and pink, the area becomes a prime spot for couples, friends, and solo travelers alike to gather and witness the mesmerizing spectacle. The vibrant colors of the houses, the tranquil lull of the waves, and the warm embrace of the fading light form a symphony of sensations that create an atmosphere perfect for quiet contemplation or shared moments.

## Panagia Paraportiani: Architectural Marvel

Mykonos Town, with its labyrinthine streets and enchanting alleys, holds a hidden architectural gem that captivates all who lay eyes upon it: the Panagia Paraportiani. Often referred to as one of Greece's most photographed churches, this stunning whitewashed structure is a living testament to the island's intricate history and artistic heritage.

The Panagia Paraportiani is not just a single building, but a fusion of several chapels constructed over different periods. This unique architectural evolution has resulted in a complex and harmonious design that's both breathtaking and distinct. The structure consists of four chapels at ground level and one at the top, each contributing to the church's distinctive asymmetrical silhouette.

As you approach the Panagia Paraportiani, the play of light and shadow on its white walls creates an ever-changing visual spectacle. Whether viewed from a distance against the azure sky or up close in the narrow alleys of Mykonos Town, the church's beauty transcends time and invokes a sense of wonder.

Stepping inside, you're met with a serene ambiance that's enhanced by the soft glow of candles and the gentle echoes of footsteps on the worn stone floor. Byzantine icons and religious artifacts adorn the interior, adding to the sense of spirituality that infuses the space. The Panagia Paraportiani's significance extends beyond its architectural marvel—it's a place of worship, reflection, and a testament to the artistic spirit of Mykonos.

## Matogianni Street: Shopping and Strolling

Amidst the sun-soaked beaches and pulsating nightlife, Matogianni Street emerges as the beating heart of Mykonos' cosmopolitan charm. This bustling thoroughfare, located in Mykonos Town, is a haven for shopping enthusiasts, culture seekers, and anyone eager to absorb the island's vibrant energy.

Lined with an array of boutiques, galleries, cafes, and restaurants, Matogianni Street offers a kaleidoscope of experiences that cater to a diverse range of tastes. Whether you're in search of fashionable clothing, unique artworks, handcrafted jewelry, or simply a leisurely spot to enjoy a cup of coffee, Matogianni Street delivers an enticing blend of options.

The street's vibrancy is palpable as locals and tourists alike weave through the crowds, exploring the charming stores that line both sides. Here, you'll find everything from international luxury brands to local artisans showcasing their craftsmanship. The spirit of Mykonos' creative community is palpable in the unique pieces on display, allowing you to take a piece of the island's essence home with you.

Matogianni Street isn't just about the shopping—it's about the experience. As you stroll along the cobblestone path, the atmosphere is alive with chatter, laughter, and the tantalizing aromas of Greek cuisine wafting from nearby eateries. It's a place where you can strike up conversations with shopkeepers, discover hidden treasures, and relish in the simple pleasure of wandering through an authentic Mediterranean scene.

## Mykonian Spiti: Culinary and Cultural Experiences

Beyond the sun-soaked beaches and iconic landmarks, there's a quieter, more intimate side of Mykonos that beckons to be explored—a side that invites you to delve into the heart of local culture and traditions. One of the most enriching ways to do this is through the Mykonian Spiti experience—an immersive culinary journey that grants you access to the homes and lives of Mykonian families.

Stepping into a Mykonian home, you're immediately embraced by the warmth and hospitality that the island is renowned for. The experience begins with a traditional home-cooked meal, prepared with love and care by the hosts. From the aroma of freshly baked bread to the rich flavors of locally sourced ingredients, each dish tells a story of Mykonos' culinary heritage.

As you dine on delectable Greek specialties, your hosts regale you with tales of Mykonos' history, customs, and way of life. The conversations are as nourishing as the food, providing a window into the island's soul beyond the typical tourist attractions. It's a chance to engage with locals, share perspectives, and forge connections that transcend cultural boundaries.

Beyond the meal, the Mykonian Spiti experience often includes traditional music and dancing, allowing you to immerse yourself in the island's vibrant culture. The melodies of bouzouki and the lively rhythms of traditional Greek dances fill the air, creating an atmosphere of celebration and camaraderie. Whether you're learning the steps or simply tapping your feet to the beat, you'll find yourself swept up in the joyous spirit of the evening.

Partaking in a Mykonian Spiti experience isn't just a culinary adventure—it's an intimate encounter with the heart and soul of Mykonos. It's a reminder that beyond the glitz and glamour, there's a community with deep-rooted traditions and a genuine desire to share their culture with those who seek a deeper connection with the places they visit. As you bid farewell to your hosts, you leave not just with a satisfied palate, but with a newfound appreciation for the island's heritage and the bonds that unite us all.

In Conclusion, Naxos, with its harmonious blend of tradition and tranquility, captivates the soul of every traveler who steps onto its shores. From the iconic silhouette of Portara to the heights of Mount Zeus and the immersive cultural experiences in between, Naxos offers a diverse array of experiences that resonate deeply. It's a place where the echoes of history mingle with the serenity of the present, creating an enchanting destination that beckons exploration and introspection.

## Paros and Antiparos: A Duo of Delights

Nestled within the heart of the Cyclades archipelago, Paros and Antiparos stand as a captivating duo that beckons travelers with their unique charm, stunning landscapes, and rich cultural heritage. These two islands, while close in proximity, offer distinct experiences that cater to a diverse range of preferences. From the bustling streets of Parikia to the serene beaches of Antiparos, this chapter delves into the enchanting exploration of Paros and Antiparos.

## Parikia and Naoussa Exploration

Parikia: Serving as the capital and main port of Paros, Parikia welcomes visitors with its harmonious blend of ancient history and modern vibrancy. As you disembark from the ferry, the sight of the town's iconic windmill and the imposing Panagia Ekatontapiliani Church immediately capture your attention. Known as the Church of 100 Doors, this architectural marvel is a testament to the island's Byzantine past. Wander through its intricate design and feel the weight of history within its walls.

The charming labyrinthine streets of Parikia are a delight to explore. Boutiques, art galleries, and traditional tavernas line the narrow passages, offering a chance to immerse yourself in local life. The Paros Archaeological Museum showcases artifacts that span millennia, shedding light on the island's ancient origins. Don't miss the chance to wander up to the Kastro, the old Venetian fortress, where panoramic views of the town and harbor unfold.

Naoussa: A short journey from Parikia takes you to the picturesque fishing village of Naoussa, an embodiment of Cycladic postcard beauty. The town's quaint harbor is a hive of activity, with colorful fishing boats bobbing on the turquoise waters. Walk along the promenade, indulging in fresh seafood at waterfront tavernas while absorbing the tranquil ambiance. The Venetian Castle, which dates back to the 15th century, offers a glimpse into the island's history and provides a stunning vantage point for sunset views.

Naoussa's nightlife is a highlight in its own right. As the sun dips below the horizon, the town's vibrant energy comes alive. Dance the night away in chic bars and clubs that line the harbor, or opt for a more relaxed atmosphere in traditional ouzerias where you can savor local mezedes (small dishes) paired with ouzo.

## Beaches, Caves, and Offbeat Escapes in Antiparos

### *Antiparos: A Tranquil Haven of Natural Beauty and Serenity*

Just a short ferry ride away from the bustling shores of Paros, the small island of Antiparos emerges as a serene oasis of tranquility and unspoiled beauty in the heart of the Cyclades. As you step off the ferry onto the shores of Antiparos, you'll be greeted by an immediate sense of calmness and the distinct lack of crowds that often characterize more popular tourist destinations. Here, time seems to slow down, inviting you to immerse yourself in the soothing rhythm of island life and embrace the true essence of relaxation.

### **Unveiling the Unblemished Beaches:**

One of the most enchanting features of Antiparos is its collection of pristine beaches, each offering a unique ambiance and an opportunity to unwind amidst nature's marvels. Psaralyki Beach stands out as a family-friendly haven, boasting soft golden sands and shallow, crystal-clear waters that gently lap at the shore. This beach is the ideal spot for families with children, as well as for those seeking a laid-back atmosphere where they can lounge under the sun or engage in leisurely swims.

For the traveler yearning for a more secluded and intimate experience, Soros Beach beckons with its untouched beauty and captivating surroundings. Nestled away from the bustle of the world, Soros Beach offers a pristine escape, where azure waters meet powdery sands, creating a scene of natural elegance. The tranquil setting invites visitors to relish in quiet contemplation, far from the noise of urban life.

### *Journeying into the Subterranean Marvel:*

Among the distinctive attractions of Antiparos, the Cave of Antiparos stands as an awe-inspiring testament to the island's geological wonders and ancient history. This underground marvel has been captivating visitors for centuries, with its labyrinthine passages and mesmerizing formations of stalactites and stalagmites. Descending into the depths of the cave is a journey into a world of captivating shapes, where nature's artistic hand has meticulously carved intricate formations that inspire awe and wonder.

The Cave of Antiparos holds a rich history, with its chambers having been explored by ancient Greek and Roman adventurers. As you traverse the cave's dimly lit passages, you'll encounter breathtaking formations that have evolved over millennia, showcasing nature's mastery and the passage of time. This subterranean excursion offers a unique perspective on the island's geological evolution and an opportunity for contemplation amidst the ancient beauty of the earth.

### *Escaping into the Unconventional:*

Antiparos goes beyond the ordinary tourist experiences, offering a plethora of offbeat and adventurous opportunities for the intrepid traveler. A hike to the Venetian Castle, perched majestically atop a hill, promises panoramic vistas that encompass the island's rugged landscapes and the expanse of the Aegean Sea. This vantage point rewards your efforts with a view that encapsulates the island's essence, making it a perfect spot for both sunrise and sunset excursions.

For a glimpse into the island's authentic Cycladic character, a visit to the traditional village of Antiparos is a must. White-washed houses adorned with bursts of vibrant blue and charming narrow alleys create an atmosphere that transports you to a simpler, more idyllic time. The village exudes a sense of tranquility that resonates with the island's overall spirit. Among its cobblestone pathways and charming squares, you'll discover local cafes, artisans' workshops, and intimate tavernas where you can savor traditional flavors and mingle with the warm-hearted locals.

The Venetian Kastro adds another layer of historical intrigue to Antiparos. This imposing structure dates back to the 15th century and provides insight into the island's rich past. As you wander through the remnants of the fortress, you'll gain a deeper understanding of the island's historical significance and its role within the region.

In the embrace of Antiparos, time slows down and the connection with nature and history deepens. Whether you're seeking the serenity of untouched beaches, the enchantment of an ancient cave, or the thrill of venturing off the beaten path, Antiparos delivers an experience that resonates with the soul of the adventurous traveler.

## Artistic Enclaves and Workshops: Nurturing Creativity in Paros and Antiparos

Beyond the sun-drenched beaches and azure waters that grace the Cyclades, a different kind of beauty thrives on the islands of Paros and Antiparos. These twin havens have emerged as artistic enclaves, attracting talents from all corners of the world to create, share, and celebrate their passion. Immerse yourself in the vibrant world of creativity as you explore Paros' Marpissa village and Antiparos' captivating art scene.

### *Paros' Marpissa: A Mural-Adorned Dream*

Marpissa, a picturesque village on Paros, offers a visual feast that transcends the ordinary. Wandering through its narrow streets, you'll find yourself surrounded by walls adorned with colorful murals and intricate artistic expressions. Every corner reveals a canvas that tells a unique story, a reflection of the island's cultural heritage and contemporary spirit. These murals often draw inspiration from mythology, history, and the natural landscape, creating a harmonious blend of tradition and innovation.

### *Antiparos' Artistic Scene: A Gallery of Talents*

Antiparos, too, is a thriving hub for artistic expression. The island's galleries and workshops showcase a diverse range of local and international talents. Whether you're drawn to traditional forms or contemporary interpretations, you'll find something that resonates with your artistic sensibilities. The galleries are not just spaces to observe art; they're interactive platforms that invite dialogue and connection. Engage with artists and gain insights into their creative process, enriching your understanding of the pieces before you.

### *Pottery and Ceramic Workshops: Crafting Timeless Pieces*

One of the most immersive ways to experience the artistic essence of Paros and Antiparos is by participating in pottery and ceramic workshops. Guided by skilled artisans, visitors have the opportunity to channel their own creative energy into shaping clay and crafting pottery. The experience is not just about creating an object; it's a journey into the tactile world of craftsmanship that has been a part of Cycladic culture for centuries. Whether you're a novice or an experienced artist, these workshops provide a space to explore, experiment, and create something truly unique.

## Sunset Sailing and Nautical Adventures: Writing Poetry on the Aegean Waters

As the sun casts its golden glow upon the Aegean Sea, another form of artistry unfolds on the waters surrounding Paros and Antiparos. Sunset sailing experiences offer a canvas of shifting hues, with the sky and sea merging in a breathtaking display of color. Embarking from Naoussa's charming harbor or Parikia's tranquil bay, you'll feel the gentle breeze against your skin as you set sail. The sun's descent becomes a symphony of color, from fiery oranges to tranquil purples, evoking a sense of serenity and wonder.

***Catamaran and Yacht Excursions: Navigating the Ethereal Waters***

Many tour operators offer catamaran and yacht excursions that provide a luxurious vantage point to witness the Aegean's beauty. These vessels offer not just a means of transportation but an experience in themselves. During your journey, you'll have the chance to explore secluded coves, where you can dive into the refreshing waters and connect with the sea's embrace. Indulge in the flavors of the Mediterranean with delectable cuisine prepared on board, enhancing the sensory feast of your nautical adventure.

## Local Festivals and Celebrations: Dancing to the Rhythm of Tradition

To truly understand the heart of a place, one must immerse themselves in its cultural fabric. Paros and Antiparos offer a myriad of local festivals and celebrations that provide an intimate glimpse into island life. Paros hosts a range of events throughout the year, from religious processions that honor saints to music festivals that celebrate both traditional and contemporary Greek melodies. These festivals not only showcase the islands' cultural richness but also invite visitors to partake in the festivities, bridging the gap between traveler and local.

### Antiparos' "Rockefeller" Festival: A Philanthropic Commemoration

Antiparos has its own unique celebrations, such as the "Rockefeller" festival, named in honor of the American millionaire's philanthropic efforts on the island. This event is a testament to the power of communal spirit, bringing people together through art, music, and cultural exchange. The festival serves as a reminder that the connection between art and community is a bridge that transcends borders and languages.

## Underwater Exploration and Diving: A Symphony of Marine Beauty

Beneath the waves that lap against Paros and Antiparos lies a world of enchantment waiting to be discovered. The Cyclades' underwater landscapes are as captivating as their terrestrial counterparts. Diving into the depths offers a chance to explore submerged caves adorned with intricate formations, encounter vibrant marine life that populates the Mediterranean, and uncover ancient shipwrecks that bear witness to the passage of time.

### Dive Centers and Courses: Plunging into the Depths

Dive centers on both islands cater to divers of all levels, from beginners seeking their first underwater experience to seasoned explorers searching for hidden treasures. These centers offer courses that provide comprehensive training and guidance, ensuring a safe and enjoyable diving experience. Whether you're discovering the underwater world for the first time or seeking to enhance your skills, the opportunity to explore the Aegean's depths is a journey into a realm of awe-inspiring beauty.

## Day Trip to Despotiko Island: Unearthing Archaeological Treasures

A short boat ride from Antiparos transports you to the uninhabited isle of Despotiko, a jewel with a rich archaeological significance. The island is famed for its ancient sanctuary dedicated to Apollo. Walking amidst the ruins, you'll feel the echoes of the past, a connection to the people who once worshipped and sought solace in this sacred space. The archaeological site is a testament to the enduring influence of art, culture, and spirituality on these islands.

### *Remote Beaches and Tranquil Ambiance: A Peaceful Escape*

Despotiko is more than its archaeological allure; it offers remote beaches and a serene ambiance that entice those seeking tranquility. The island's untouched beauty serves as a backdrop for relaxation and contemplation. As you wander along the shoreline, the gentle lapping of the waves and the distant cry of seagulls become a soundtrack to your escape, inviting you to immerse yourself in the natural rhythms of the island.

In conclusion, the artistic enclaves and captivating adventures found on Paros and Antiparos offer a multi-faceted exploration of creativity, beauty, and cultural immersion. From pottery workshops that allow you to shape your artistic vision to sunset sails that paint poetry on the Aegean canvas, from local festivals that bring communities together to underwater explorations that unveil the secrets of the sea, and from archaeological treasures on Despotiko Island to the tranquil escape it offers—these islands beckon travelers to uncover the artistic and natural wonders that lie within their embrace.

In conclusion, Paros and Antiparos form a dynamic duo within the Cyclades, each offering its own unique blend of history, culture, and natural beauty. Whether you're wandering through the streets of Parikia and Naoussa, lounging on the serene beaches of Antiparos, or exploring hidden caves and offbeat villages, these islands promise an unforgettable journey that captures the essence of the Cycladic experience.

# Milos: Hidden Treasures in the Cyclades

Nestled among the Cyclades, the island of Milos is a captivating destination that often remains undiscovered by the crowds. While its more renowned neighbors may steal the limelight, Milos boasts a unique allure of its own with a diverse landscape, rich history, and a sense of serenity that enchants every traveler who steps ashore.

## Sarakiniko's Moon-Like Landscape

One of the most surreal and distinctive features of Milos is the otherworldly Sarakiniko Beach. Often described as a lunar landscape, Sarakiniko's dramatic white volcanic rock formations create an ethereal atmosphere that seems straight out of a science fiction movie. As you walk along the smooth, curved surfaces, you'll be surrounded by a landscape that appears as if it were sculpted by the hands of an artist with a penchant for the abstract.

The beach's moon-like appearance is the result of volcanic activity that shaped Milos millions of years ago. The natural erosion of the volcanic rock has crafted stunning formations that are perfect for exploration and photography. The interplay between the bright white rock, the crystal-clear blue waters, and the vivid azure sky provides an extraordinary backdrop for memorable pictures and a meditative escape.

## Catacombs, Sea Caves, and Sulphur Springs

Beyond Sarakiniko, Milos continues to reveal its hidden treasures. The island's history dates back to ancient times, and its rich archaeological sites bear testament to the civilizations that once thrived here. One such fascinating site is the Catacombs of Milos, a complex of underground burial chambers that is among the most important Christian monuments in Greece. These catacombs provide a glimpse into the early Christian era and are a reminder of the island's historical significance.

Exploring Milos wouldn't be complete without venturing into its sea caves, and the island boasts some of the most captivating ones in the Cyclades. Kleftiko, reachable only by boat, is a series of sea caves that have been carved by the relentless waves and winds over centuries. The turquoise waters that surround the caves invite snorkelers and divers to discover the marine life thriving beneath the surface.

Adding to the island's allure are its sulphur springs, which offer a unique and therapeutic experience. The naturally occurring springs are said to have healing properties, making a visit to these warm and mineral-rich waters not only relaxing but also beneficial for your skin and overall well-being. The sulphur springs are particularly popular in the village of Adamas, where you can take a soothing dip and enjoy the natural spa-like environment.

Milos, unlike its more bustling counterparts, offers a serene escape where you can unwind and immerse yourself in nature's wonders. It's a place where you can explore hidden corners, find tranquil spots for contemplation, and engage with the island's rich history and geology. Whether you're strolling along the lunar landscape of Sarakiniko, delving into the ancient catacombs, exploring sea caves by boat, or indulging in the rejuvenating sulphur springs, Milos presents a world of adventure and relaxation that caters to every traveler's desires.

## Milos Mining Museum: Unearthing the Island's Industrial Past

Deep within the layers of Milos' history lies an enthralling narrative of mining and the island's profound mineral wealth. The Milos Mining Museum stands as a gateway to this rich past, offering visitors an immersive journey into the island's long-standing mining heritage. Nestled within an unassuming building, the museum is a treasure trove of knowledge and artifacts that unveil the pivotal role minerals played in shaping Milos' identity.

As you step into the museum, you're immediately transported back in time to an era when minerals were not just resources but the backbone of the island's economy. The exhibits meticulously chronicle the tools, equipment, and techniques that were integral to the mineral extraction industry. From obsidian, the volcanic glass used in tools and weaponry, to kaolin, the fine clay that found its way into ceramics and cosmetics, the museum sheds light on the diverse array of valuable resources that Milos once provided to the world.

But the museum's value extends beyond the geological and economic aspects. It narrates a tale of labor, craftsmanship, and the resilience of the people who toiled to extract these precious materials from the earth. Interactive displays allow visitors to understand the intricacies of the extraction process, giving a firsthand experience of the challenges faced by the miners.

What sets the Milos Mining Museum apart is its ability to paint a vivid picture of the island's economic and social landscape through the ages. It showcases the evolution of mining techniques, the influence of various civilizations on the island's mining practices, and the profound impact of these activities on Milos' communities.

By delving into Milos' mining history, the museum not only uncovers a forgotten chapter of the island's past but also imparts a deeper understanding of its cultural and economic significance. It is a testament to the resilience, resourcefulness, and ingenuity of the people who once shaped Milos' destiny through their tireless efforts in the mines.

Visiting the Milos Mining Museum is not just an educational experience—it's an opportunity to connect with the island's roots and appreciate the untold stories that have contributed to its present-day character. As you walk through its exhibits, you'll gain a newfound appreciation for the hidden treasures that lay beneath the surface of Milos, both in terms of its geological wealth and the enduring spirit of its people.

From the geological marvels to the human stories, the Milos Mining Museum brings to light the layers of history that continue to resonate in the present and enrich the island's identity. It's a place where visitors can unearth the past and forge a connection with the island's industrial heritage that's often hidden from the casual traveler's eye.

## Firopotamos: A Quaint Fishing Village by the Sea

Nestled along the rugged coastline of Milos, the picturesque village of Firopotamos emerges as a tranquil haven that embodies the essence of traditional Cycladic life. As you approach this idyllic hamlet, you're greeted by a scene straight out of a postcard: whitewashed buildings adorned with vibrant blue doors and windows, standing in harmonious contrast against the azure sea and the clear sky.

Firopotamos, with its modest size and unpretentious charm, offers a refreshing escape from the bustling tourist spots found on some other Cycladic islands. This quiet fishing village exudes an air of authenticity, allowing visitors to experience the island's traditional way of life in its purest form.

What sets Firopotamos apart is its unique layout. The buildings cluster around a small bay, creating a cozy amphitheater-like setting that seems to have been designed with both practicality and aesthetics in mind. The bay's calm and shallow crystalline waters are perfect for leisurely swims and moments of relaxation. Colorful fishing boats gently sway in the gentle currents, casting picturesque reflections on the water's surface.

One of the village's distinctive features is the presence of quaint boat garages, carved directly into the rock to protect the fishermen's vessels from the elements. These charming structures provide a glimpse into the close relationship between the residents and the sea, emphasizing the village's historical reliance on fishing as a way of life.

While the village is relatively untouched by the bustling tourism that characterizes some other parts of Milos, it hasn't remained completely immune to the needs of modern travelers. A few local taverns offer a taste of Milos' traditional cuisine, allowing you to savor fresh seafood and other local delicacies against the backdrop of the Aegean Sea.

Whether you're seeking a serene spot for reflection, a chance to experience genuine Cycladic culture, or simply a place to take in stunning coastal views, Firopotamos delivers on all fronts. As you meander through its narrow lanes and enjoy the simplicity of life by the sea, you'll find that Firopotamos captures the essence of the Cyclades' understated beauty—one that speaks to the heart and leaves an indelible impression of tranquility and authenticity.

Firopotamos is a hidden treasure that beckons travelers to step away from the ordinary and immerse themselves in a world where time seems to slow down. It offers an opportunity to connect with the island's heritage, to engage with the local community, and to find solace in the unspoiled beauty of Milos' coastline. For those seeking a respite from the hustle and bustle, Firopotamos stands as a quintessential Cycladic escape that's waiting to be discovered.

# Plaka: Exploring Milos' Enchanting Capital

Perched atop a gentle hill overlooking the Aegean Sea, the enchanting capital of Milos, Plaka, beckons travelers with its timeless beauty and captivating charm. As you ascend its winding streets, you're transported into a world where whitewashed houses, cobblestone pathways, and stunning vistas converge to create an experience that feels like stepping into a Cycladic dream.

Plaka's architectural splendor is a feast for the eyes. The traditional Cycladic design is evident in every corner, with narrow alleys flanked by buildings adorned in the iconic white facades and blue accents that define the island's aesthetic. Flowers in vibrant hues spill over terraces and balconies, infusing the air with a sweet fragrance and adding a touch of nature to the stone-paved lanes.

The heart of Plaka is dominated by the Venetian Castle, an imposing structure that stands as a testament to the island's historical significance. Wandering through the castle's remnants, you'll encounter sweeping panoramas that offer a bird's-eye view of Milos' rugged coastline, the azure sea, and the scattered Cycladic islands in the distance. The sunset paints the sky with warm hues, transforming the castle's surroundings into an ethereal canvas that's perfect for romantic strolls or quiet contemplation.

While Plaka exudes an air of tranquility, it's also a hub of cultural vibrancy. Quaint taverns and charming boutiques are interspersed throughout the village, offering opportunities to savor local cuisine and shop for handmade crafts and souvenirs. The cultural scene is further enriched by museums and galleries that highlight the island's history, art, and heritage.

As daylight fades and the stars emerge, Plaka transforms into a realm of enchantment. The village's labyrinthine streets come alive with the soft glow of lanterns, casting whimsical shadows on the walls. The local taverns and cafes radiate a warm ambiance, inviting you to savor authentic Greek dishes and engage in leisurely conversations with both locals and fellow travelers.

Plaka's allure lies not only in its physical beauty but also in the way it immerses visitors in the soul of Milos. With every step, you're surrounded by the echoes of the past and the spirit of the present—a fusion that creates an experience that's both immersive and enlightening. Plaka serves as a bridge between history and modernity, offering a space where you can embrace the island's cultural richness while finding your own place within its narrative.

For those seeking an exploration of Milos beyond its natural wonders, Plaka is a destination that captures the essence of the Cyclades. Its narrow streets lead to broader horizons, its historical sites whisper tales of time gone by, and its welcoming atmosphere invites you to participate in the rhythms of local life. Whether you're captivated by its panoramic views, charmed by its architecture, or intrigued by its cultural offerings, Plaka is a captivating gem that's sure to leave an indelible mark on your Cycladic journey.

# Ancient Theater of Milos: A Step into the Past

Nestled within the embrace of Milos' scenic landscape, the Ancient Theater stands as a testament to the island's rich history and its enduring connection with the arts. Carved into the natural slope of the land, this archaeological marvel dates back to the Hellenistic period, serving as a vibrant hub for cultural gatherings and performances that once resonated through the ancient Greek world.

Approaching the theater, you're met with a sense of awe as the tiers of stone seats gradually come into view. Each row represents a piece of history, a place where generations of spectators once sat, transfixed by the theatrical and musical performances that unfolded on the stage. Even now, the acoustics of the theater's design continue to echo the applause, laughter, and melodies of bygone eras.

Walking through the well-preserved passages and stairways, you can almost hear the echoes of the actors, musicians, and audiences that once animated this space. From grand tragedies to lively comedies, the Ancient Theater was a canvas for the ancient Greeks to explore the breadth of human emotions and experiences. The seating arrangement itself tells a story of social hierarchy, as the prominent positions were reserved for the privileged, while the less fortunate occupied the higher tiers.

But the true magic of the Ancient Theater lies not just in its historical significance, but also in its integration with the natural landscape. As you take a seat and let your gaze sweep across the horizon, you're greeted with panoramic views that stretch out to the sparkling Aegean Sea. The theater becomes a nexus between human creativity and the beauty of the surrounding world, as though the architecture itself seeks to bridge the gap between the artistic and the divine.

For modern visitors, the Ancient Theater offers a unique opportunity to step back in time. Sitting in the stone seats, you can envision the vibrant performances that once captivated audiences, the stories that unfolded on the stage, and the collective emotions that surged through the crowd. It's a poignant reminder of the enduring power of art to transcend time and connect people across the ages.

In exploring the Ancient Theater of Milos, you're not merely encountering a historical site—you're engaging with a living testament to the human spirit. It's a space where the past and the present coalesce, where the arts and nature converge, and where the stories of ancient civilizations intertwine with your own journey. Whether you're a history enthusiast, an art lover, or simply a traveler seeking to immerse yourself in the magic of the Cyclades, the Ancient Theater of Milos beckons you to embark on a remarkable journey through time and culture.

## Tsigrado Beach: A Secluded Cove of Tranquility

In the realm of hidden treasures on Milos, Tsigrado Beach stands as a symbol of seclusion and untouched beauty. Accessible only through a somewhat daring adventure down a cliffside with the aid of ropes and ladders, this pristine cove is a haven for intrepid explorers seeking a tranquil escape from the outside world.

As you make your way down the rugged path that leads to Tsigrado Beach, a sense of anticipation builds. The path's descent takes you through a narrow crevice in the rock, revealing glimpses of the crystal-clear sea below. Upon reaching the sandy shores, you're greeted with a sight that seems almost surreal: a small, secluded beach nestled within towering cliffs, surrounded by the gentle lapping of turquoise waters.

The cove's sheltered location makes it a sanctuary of serenity. The towering cliffs that encircle Tsigrado create a natural amphitheater, where the sound of the waves and the rustling of the breeze are amplified, creating a soothing symphony that envelops the senses. Soft, powdery sands offer a comfortable spot for relaxation, while the clear waters invite you to indulge in leisurely swims and underwater exploration.

The sense of isolation and exclusivity that Tsigrado offers is unparalleled. The journey to reach the beach, while requiring a certain level of adventurous spirit, contributes to its untouched allure. The absence of roads and large crowds fosters an environment of tranquility, allowing you to unwind, reflect, and bask in the simplicity of nature.

The towering cliffs also hold another gem—a sea cave that beckons explorers to delve further into Tsigrado's secrets. Venturing into the cave, you'll discover an ethereal world illuminated by the soft glow of the sun filtering through gaps in the rock. The cave's interior is a magical place for those who seek to connect with the island's geology and history in an intimate and awe-inspiring manner.

Tsigrado Beach is a reminder that amidst the bustling energy of the Cyclades, there are still places where time seems to stand still. It's an invitation to step off the beaten path, to embrace the raw beauty of nature, and to experience a sense of solitude that's becoming increasingly rare in today's world. For those willing to take the journey, Tsigrado is a hidden cove of tranquility where you can savor the unspoiled wonder of Milos' coastal paradise and create lasting memories of a true Cycladic escape.

In conclusion, Milos stands as a testament to the diversity and magnificence of the Cyclades. From the enchanting moon-like landscapes of Sarakiniko to the intriguing catacombs that tell tales of the past, and from the exploration of sea caves to the indulgence in sulphur springs, the island offers a tapestry of experiences that few destinations can match. For those seeking a quieter, more intimate encounter with the Cyclades, Milos is a hidden gem waiting to be discovered.

# Chapter 4: Soaking in Cycladic Culture and Cuisine

## Gastronomic Journey: Savoring Authentic Cycladic Delicacies

The Cycladic culinary scene is a journey through history, geography, and culture, encapsulating the very essence of the islands themselves. As you embark on this gastronomic adventure, prepare to be dazzled by flavors that mirror the vibrant hues of the Aegean Sea and the sun-soaked landscapes. This chapter invites you to uncover the fusion of Mediterranean ingredients and local traditions that have shaped Cycladic cuisine into a symphony of tastes and aromas.

**Embracing Tradition and Fusion**

Cycladic cuisine stands as a testament to the islands' rich history, where the flavors on your plate are a tapestry woven with threads of ancient traditions and diverse cultural influences. Imagine the culinary landscape as a mosaic, with each tile representing a different era and civilization that has left its imprint on the Cyclades. From the time of Ancient Greece to the Byzantine era, Ottoman rule, and the Venetian period, these islands have been a melting pot of cultures, and their food reflects this dynamic history.

As you savor the dishes, you're tasting the stories of these interactions—a symphony of culinary experiences that have been handed down through generations. Every bite holds a piece of this complex narrative, a journey that bridges time and geography. Yet, what makes Cycladic cuisine truly exceptional is its ability to preserve individual identities while welcoming new ingredients and techniques, creating a harmonious blend of tradition and innovation.

**Fresh Herbs, Olive Oil, and Local Bounty**

In the heart of Cycladic cuisine lies an unwavering respect for the land's bounty. The islands' arid climate and rugged landscape have spurred a culinary ingenuity that transforms scarcity into abundance. Here, fresh herbs like oregano, thyme, and rosemary are not just seasonings—they're storytellers. Their fragrances evoke the sun-drenched hillsides, while their flavors infuse every dish with a distinct, aromatic essence. These herbs thrive despite the challenging conditions, embodying the resilience of the islanders themselves.

And then there's olive oil—the golden elixir that ties the Mediterranean diet together. It flows like a river through Cycladic kitchens, enriching flavors, and imparting a smooth, velvety texture to dishes. Its presence is a reminder of the deep connection between these islands and the olive trees that have stood as guardians of tradition for centuries.

**Limited Resources, Rich Flavors**

The Cyclades' topography, defined by rocky terrain and scarce arable land, has nurtured an approach to cooking that turns limitations into strengths. Islanders have learned to transform humble ingredients into culinary triumphs. Chickpeas and fava beans, known as "revithia" and "fava," respectively, take center stage in dishes that resonate with nourishment and authenticity. These legumes, born from the earth's challenges, become canvases for creativity, showcasing the islanders' ability to make the most of what they have.

Creative techniques elevate even the most basic ingredients. Dishes like "Kopanisti," a tangy cheese spread with chili peppers, embody this resourcefulness. This spread, born from the need to preserve cheese, now graces tables as a symbol of the Cycladic ability to turn necessity into culinary innovation.

**Seafood Delicacies: A Treasure Trove of Flavors**

The Aegean Sea, with its azure depths, dances with life, and the islands' relationship with the sea runs deep. Islanders have mastered the art of preparing seafood in ways that honor its purity. Sun-dried mackerel, known as "Gouna," emerges as a delicacy infused with olive oil and zesty lemon—a testament to the islanders' ability to capture the essence of the sea's gifts. "Astakomakaronada," a luxurious lobster pasta, encapsulates the islands' reverence for marine bounty, transforming it into a culinary experience that celebrates both sustenance and indulgence.

**Preserving Culinary Heritage**

Cycladic cuisine is more than just a menu; it's a living heritage. Through local festivals and celebrations, the islands ensure that ancient recipes remain vibrant and relevant. When you taste these dishes, you're not just indulging in flavors—you're joining a continuum that spans centuries. Participating in the rituals of the Cyclades through food means becoming part of a tradition that has transcended time, connecting you with the islanders who have, for generations, crafted meals that honor the past while embracing the present.

## Seafood Specialties and Island-Infused Flavors

The Cyclades, a collection of idyllic islands scattered like pearls in the cerulean embrace of the Aegean Sea, have always been inexorably linked to the bounty of the ocean. This unique geographical position has bestowed upon the Cyclades a culinary legacy where seafood reigns supreme, occupying a place of honor in their gastronomic tapestry.

**A Bountiful Harvest from the Depths**

As you traverse the Cycladic archipelago, you're invited to immerse yourself in a world where seafood takes center stage. The local cuisine thrives on a wealth of offerings from the Aegean waters, where fish, squid, octopus, and other maritime treasures are reeled in with care and reverence. The tradition of harvesting seafood here has deep historical roots, interwoven with the culture and livelihood of the islanders.

## Unveiling Traditional Fishing Methods

Intriguingly, the techniques employed in fishing around the Cyclades have evolved over centuries, adapting to the rhythm of the sea and the seasons. On islands like Mykonos, you might encounter the art of "sardine lampuki," where fishing vessels equipped with lanterns lure sardines towards the surface during the night. This practice not only harks back to ancient methods but also encapsulates the intimate relationship between the Cyclades and the sea.

## Economic Significance and Local Identity

Beyond their gustatory appeal, these fishing methods hold immense economic significance for the local communities. Fishing has historically been a cornerstone of the Cycladic economy, providing livelihoods to generations. It's not just a trade; it's a way of life, a connection to the past, and a binding force that knits together the fabric of the islands. When you savor the seafood on your plate, you're partaking in a tradition that echoes across time and sustains the islanders' way of living.

## Marinating and Grilling: A Culinary Artistry

The culinary prowess of the Cyclades lies not only in the selection of seafood but also in the delicate dance of flavors that ensues. Enter the realm of marinating and grilling, where the freshest catch is transformed into sublime dishes that pay homage to the sea. Traditional recipes often involve

marinating the seafood in a mixture of olive oil, lemon juice, local herbs like oregano and thyme, and a pinch of sea salt.
Grilling takes place on open fires or over hot coals, imparting a smoky essence that evokes the maritime landscape. The process is a symphony of precision, where the searing heat interacts with the marinade, conjuring aromas that tell tales of the salty sea breeze and the sun-drenched cliffs. The result? Succulent squid that yield with tenderness, octopus that boasts a sublime char, and fish that flakes apart with the mere touch of a fork.

**A Culinary Connection to the Cycladic Essence**

With each bite, you're not just savoring a meal; you're embracing the essence of the Cyclades themselves. The flavors encapsulate the very spirit of these islands—untamed, vibrant, and deeply intertwined with the rhythms of nature. The seafood on your plate embodies the union of land and sea, a testament to the resourcefulness of island life and the harmonious relationship the islanders share with their surroundings.

In the Cyclades, dining on seafood is not just an act of sustenance; it's a celebration of tradition, an homage to history, and a communion with the elements. As you embark on this culinary journey through the maritime wonders of the Aegean, you're beckoned to delve beyond the plate and into the stories of those who have nurtured this connection for generations.

# Must-Try Dishes and Recommended Restaurants

## Must-Try Dishes When in the Cyclades

When exploring the Cyclades, the culinary journey is just as enchanting as the scenic landscapes and white-washed villages. Here are 13 must-try dishes that encapsulate the vibrant flavors and cultural richness of this captivating Greek island group.

**Souvlaki:**
Souvlaki is a beloved Greek classic that transcends regions and has become a global favorite. The word "souvlaki" actually means "skewer" in Greek. It features tender pieces of meat, often marinated in olive oil, lemon juice, oregano, and other Mediterranean herbs. The meat is skewered and grilled to perfection, infusing it with smoky flavors. Served wrapped in warm pita bread, souvlaki is accompanied by vibrant and crisp fresh vegetables, such as tomatoes, onions, and lettuce. Topped with creamy tzatziki sauce, a blend of yogurt, cucumber, garlic, and dill, this portable delight is not only a quick and satisfying meal but also a taste of Greek hospitality.

**Gyro:**
Similar to souvlaki, the gyro is a Greek street food favorite that has gained worldwide popularity. The meat, often pork or chicken, is roasted on a vertical rotisserie, allowing it to cook slowly and baste in its own juices. Once cooked, the meat is thinly sliced and piled into a fluffy pita bread. This

flavorful and juicy meat is then complemented with toppings like sliced onions, tomatoes, and sometimes even French fries, creating a harmonious blend of textures and flavors. Tzatziki or other sauces are drizzled over the meat before the pita is folded into a convenient and delicious handheld meal.

**Dakos**:
Dakos is a dish that harks back to the island's rustic roots. It consists of a base made from barley rusk, a dense and dry bread made from barley flour. The rusk is softened by drizzling it with olive oil and often a splash of water. Diced tomatoes, ripe and bursting with flavor, are generously spread over the rusk. The dish is further adorned with crumbled feta cheese, olives, capers, and a finishing touch of aromatic extra virgin olive oil. Dakos encapsulates the essence of Cycladic simplicity, showcasing the island's reliance on natural and straightforward ingredients.

**Melitinia**:
Melitinia are sweet cheese pastries that showcase the Cyclades' affinity for dairy products. Made with soft myzithra cheese, a traditional Greek cheese similar to ricotta, melitinia are enriched with semolina and sugar. The dough is shaped into small boats, reminiscent of the maritime culture of the islands. These pastries are baked until they attain a golden hue, resulting in a delicate and slightly crunchy outer layer that gives way to a creamy, cheese-infused center. To enhance their sweetness, melitinia are drizzled with honey, offering a harmonious contrast of flavors that tantalize the palate.

**Revithada:**

Revithada is a dish that encapsulates comfort and nourishment. The humble chickpea stew is a staple of Cycladic cuisine, made by slow-cooking chickpeas with onions, olive oil, and an assortment of aromatic herbs. The result is a hearty and flavorful stew that reflects the region's reliance on locally sourced and readily available ingredients. Revithada is a testament to the art of creating deeply satisfying dishes with simplicity and a touch of culinary creativity. This dish warms both body and soul, offering a taste of the island's traditional comfort food.

**Astakomakaronada:**
Astakomakaronada is a testament to the Cyclades' connection to the Aegean Sea. This seafood pasta dish features fresh lobster, a prized delicacy harvested from the azure waters surrounding the islands. The lobster is combined with pasta and simmered in a rich tomato-based sauce, infusing the dish with both the flavors of the sea and the land. Astakomakaronada highlights the Cycladic devotion to marrying local ingredients and traditions, resulting in a dish that celebrates the bounty of the Aegean Sea.

**Bakaliaros Skordalia:**
Bakaliaros Skordalia is a dish that showcases the islanders' ingenuity in utilizing preserved ingredients. Salted codfish, known as "bakaliaros," is deep-fried to create a crispy exterior that contrasts with the tender and flavorful interior. It is traditionally served with skordalia, a garlicky potato and olive oil dip. The creaminess of skordalia complements the textural play of the fried codfish, creating a harmonious marriage of flavors and a satisfying interplay of textures.

This dish is a popular choice for both appetizers and main courses, reflecting its versatility and the Cyclades' ability to transform simple ingredients into delectable creations.

**Kopanisti:**

Kopanisti is a fiery cheese spread that tantalizes the taste buds with its robust flavors. Made from local cheeses like feta and myzithra, kopanisti is elevated with the addition of red pepper flakes, resulting in a tangy, creamy, and spicy concoction. The Cyclades are known for their spicy and robust foods, and kopanisti embodies this culinary spirit. Perfect for spreading on bread or dipping with vegetables, this spicy cheese spread adds a delightful kick to any meal and provides a sensory journey through Cycladic flavors.

**Kavourmas:**

Kavourmas is a savory delight that showcases the islanders' resourcefulness in preserving meat. Pork or lamb is slow-cooked in its own fat, resulting in tender and flavorful meat that can be stored for extended periods. The meat is often seasoned with fragrant herbs and spices, infusing it with a rich aroma and taste. Kavourmas is typically enjoyed as a spread on bread, adding a burst of flavor to each bite. It's also a star in mezze platters, inviting diners to experience the Cycladic dedication to creating dishes that combine tradition, taste, and practicality.

**Louza:**

Louza is an air-dried and seasoned pork delicacy that speaks to the island's culinary heritage. The pork is carefully prepared, seasoned with aromatic herbs, and then air-dried to create a flavorful cold cut. The thin slices of louza are tender and full of taste, making them a popular addition to mezze platters. Often featured alongside other cured meats and cheeses, louza offers a glimpse into the islanders' techniques for preserving meats and crafting flavors that celebrate the passage of time.

## Patatato:

Patatato is a hearty stew that exemplifies the islanders' ability to create delicious and fulfilling dishes using locally available ingredients. Chunks of beef or goat are slow-cooked to tender perfection alongside potatoes and a medley of fragrant spices. The result is a dish that encapsulates the essence of comfort food, inviting diners to savor the rich flavors and aroma. Patatato is a celebration of Cycladic cuisine's ability to transform simple components into a dish that warms the heart and evokes a sense of community and tradition.

## Fava:

Cycladic fava is a creamy puree made from split yellow peas. This dish showcases the island's creativity in utilizing legumes to create a nutritious and flavorful delicacy. The split peas are slow-cooked until they break down into a smooth and velvety consistency. Cycladic fava is often drizzled with aromatic olive oil, adorned with capers and onions, and served as a dip or spread. It offers a balance of texture and taste that delights the senses while underscoring the Cyclades' focus on creating dishes that are both nourishing and delicious.

## Amygdalota:

Amygdalota are almond cookies that tantalize the palate with their delicate sweetness. These delightful treats are often enjoyed with a cup of Greek coffee or served as a dessert after a satisfying meal. Made from ground almonds, sugar, and a hint of rose water, amygdalota capture the essence of Cycladic sweetness and the region's connection to the Mediterranean's abundant almond trees. With their fragrant aroma and melt-in-your-mouth texture, amygdalota provide a satisfying finale to any meal, leaving a lasting impression of the Cyclades' indulgent culinary heritage.

Exploring the Cyclades isn't just about stunning vistas; it's about indulging in the diverse and flavorful cuisine that paints a vivid picture of island life. With these must-try dishes, you'll savor the essence of the Cyclades, one bite at a time.

## Recommended Restaurants in the Cyclades

### Restaurant: SeaBreeze Taverna

Location: Fira, Santorini
Description: Overlooking the Caldera, SeaBreeze Taverna offers a romantic atmosphere with stunning sunset views. Enjoy traditional Greek dishes like grilled octopus and moussaka while sipping local wines. The ambiance and exquisite flavors create a memorable dining experience.

### Restaurant: Kastro Tavern

Location: Mykonos Town, Mykonos
Description: Tucked within the labyrinthine streets of Mykonos Town, Kastro Tavern is a local favorite. Sample

their "Louza" – cured pork with aromatic herbs – and revel in the cozy Cycladic ambiance. The restaurant's authenticity and friendly service stand out.

***Restaurant: Axiotissa***

Location: Chora, Naxos
Description: Axiotissa offers a fusion of Cycladic and Mediterranean flavors, served in a charming courtyard setting. Taste their "Aplomata" – slow-cooked beef with wine and herbs – and experience the genuine warmth of Naxian hospitality.

***Restaurant: Mediterraneo***

Location: Parikia, Paros
Description: Mediterraneo boasts a seafront location and a diverse menu. Try their "Astakomakaronada" – lobster pasta – for a taste of Cycladic elegance. The sea breeze and artistic decor contribute to a memorable dining setting.

***Restaurant: O! Hamos***

Location: Antiparos Town, Antiparos
Description: O! Hamos is a hidden gem serving mouthwatering dishes like "Kakavia" – fisherman's soup. Set in a traditional Cycladic house, it offers an intimate and authentic experience, showcasing the island's culinary heritage.

***Restaurant: Armenaki Taverna***

Location: Pollonia, Milos
Description: Armenaki Taverna offers delectable seafood by the beach, with the freshest catches and local produce. Try

their "Fourtalia," a local omelette, and relish the family-friendly atmosphere and panoramic sea views.

### *Restaurant: To Perasma*

Location: Naoussa, Paros
Description: Nestled in a charming alley, To Perasma offers a fusion of traditional and contemporary Greek cuisine. Savor their "Garides Saganaki" – shrimp cooked in tomato and feta – while embracing the intimate and lively ambience.

### *Restaurant: Selene*

Location: Pyrgos, Santorini
Description: Selene offers a refined gastronomic experience with an emphasis on Cycladic ingredients. Indulge in their tasting menu that highlights local flavors in innovative ways. The elegant setting and panoramic views elevate your dining journey.

### *Restaurant: Captains*

Location: Oia, Santorini
Description: Captains provides a prime sunset-viewing spot alongside delicious dishes. Their "Santorinian Salad" features cherry tomatoes and capers, reflecting the island's flavors. The terrace seating offers a front-row seat to Santorini's famed sunsets.

### *Restaurant: Ostria*

Location: Piso Livadi, Paros

Description: Ostria boasts a beachfront location, making it an ideal spot to enjoy "Athenian-style" fish and seafood. Their grilled calamari and welcoming atmosphere capture the essence of Cycladic dining.

### Restaurant: Lucky's Souvlakis

Location: Mykonos Town, Mykonos
Description: For a casual culinary experience, visit Lucky's Souvlakis. Savor traditional Greek souvlaki wraps with a modern twist. The vibrant atmosphere and quick service cater to tourists and locals alike.

### Restaurant: Lefkes Taverna

Location: Lefkes, Paros
Description: Lefkes Taverna offers a mountain village setting and traditional Greek dishes. Delight in "Lamb Kleftiko," tender lamb slow-cooked with herbs, while enjoying the rustic charm and hospitality.

### Restaurant: Metaxy Mas

Location: Exo Gonia, Santorini
Description: Metaxy Mas delivers authentic flavors in a charming courtyard. Relish their "Fava Santorinis," a local split pea puree, and soak in the rustic surroundings that reflect the heart of Santorini.

### Restaurant: To Apano Kima

Location: Plaka, Naxos

Description: To Apano Kima offers a serene beachfront experience. Enjoy grilled seafood and local specialties, such as "Kitron" – a citrus liqueur unique to Naxos. The laid-back ambiance captures the island's spirit.

### *Restaurant: Apaggio*

Location: Ornos Beach, Mykonos
Description: Apaggio is a beachfront haven where you can relish Mediterranean dishes with a modern twist. Try their "Seafood Orzotto" – a seafood-infused barley risotto – while lounging by the sea.

Exploring these recommended restaurants will take you on a culinary journey through the Cyclades, offering a diverse range of flavors, settings, and experiences that showcase the islands' unique charm and gastronomic heritage.

As you journey through this chapter, you'll uncover the heart and soul of Cycladic culture through its architecture, customs, and, most notably, its cuisine. The flavors and traditions of the Cyclades will leave an indelible mark on your travel experience, making it not only a visual feast but a sensory delight that connects you with the essence of these captivating islands.

# Chapter 5: Activities and Adventures

When visiting the Cyclades, there's no shortage of activities and adventures to engage in. Whether you're seeking relaxation on pristine beaches, embarking on scenic hikes, exploring the underwater world, or immersing yourself in the rich history of the islands, the Cyclades have something for every traveler's preference.

## Basking in the Sun: Cyclades' Top Beach Escapes

The Cyclades are renowned for their stunning beaches, each offering its own unique charm and character. Here are some must-visit beach destinations:

**Santorini's Red Beach: A Geological Marvel and Rust-Hued Oasis**

Nestled on the southern coast of Santorini, the Red Beach is a true testament to nature's artistry, where rust-colored sands meet the deep blue waters of the Aegean Sea. This iconic beach is a geological wonder, shaped by the island's volcanic history and dramatic landscape. As visitors approach the beach, they are met with a striking contrast between the vibrant red cliffs that frame the shore and the serene azure sea that stretches beyond.

The beach's unique color palette is a result of the rich iron content present in the volcanic rocks that encompass it. Over centuries, the rocks have weathered and eroded, creating a mosaic of red hues that lend the beach its distinctive name. The sands, warm to the touch, are a fascinating blend of red, orange, and maroon, creating a visually captivating scene against the backdrop of Santorini's caldera.

The experience of visiting Red Beach is more than just a visual spectacle; it's a multisensory journey. The earthy aroma of the volcanic sands, the gentle caress of the sea breeze, and the soothing sound of the waves crashing against the shore create a harmonious symphony of sensations. While swimming is possible, the strong currents and steep drop-offs make it essential to exercise caution. Many visitors prefer to bask in the sun on the beach's unique sands, capturing the essence of this geological marvel through their senses and lenses.

## Mykonos' Psarou Beach: Luxury, Leisure, and Lively Atmosphere

Mykonos is often synonymous with vibrant nightlife and luxurious beachside escapades, and Psarou Beach encapsulates this spirit perfectly. Tucked away on the island's southwestern coast, Psarou is renowned for its upscale beach clubs, inviting azure waters, and an atmosphere that seamlessly blends relaxation and sociability.

The beach's allure lies not only in its crystal-clear waters but also in the lavish beachfront establishments that line its shores. These exclusive beach clubs offer sun loungers, cabanas, and umbrellas, creating a plush haven where visitors can unwind in style. It's not uncommon to see glamorous yachts anchored just offshore, adding to the air of sophistication that pervades the scene.

Psarou Beach is a hub of activity, where beachgoers can indulge in refreshing cocktails, relish delectable Mediterranean cuisine, and mingle with fellow travelers. The sound of laughter, the clinking of glasses, and the rhythmic beats of music create an energetic ambiance that persists from day to night. While the beach is synonymous with luxury, its innate beauty and inviting waters are accessible to all, making it a must-visit for anyone seeking a taste of Mykonos' quintessential charm.

## Paros' Kolymbithres Beach: Nature's Sculpture Garden by the Sea

In the heart of Paros lies Kolymbithres Beach, a hidden gem characterized by its fascinating granite rock formations that resemble natural sculptures. As visitors approach the shore, they are greeted by a series of coves and pools created by the worn granite boulders that have been shaped by wind and water over millennia. These formations not only provide privacy and shade but also create natural swimming pools, making Kolymbithres a playground for families, adventurers, and explorers alike.

The beach's name, "Kolymbithres," translates to "small swimming pools," and it aptly captures the essence of this picturesque destination. Each cove presents a new adventure, with rocks acting as diving platforms and snorkeling spots. The translucent waters teem with marine life, inviting snorkelers to discover the vibrant underwater world. Exploring the labyrinthine rock formations and enjoying the interplay of light and shadows becomes a mesmerizing journey of discovery.

Amidst the rugged beauty, Kolymbithres offers tranquil pockets of relaxation, where visitors can bask in the sun or take refuge in the natural shade provided by the sculpted rocks. The beach's unique topography, combined with the turquoise waters of the Aegean, creates a magical ambiance that feels like a scene from a fantasy novel, beckoning travelers to immerse themselves in its enchanting embrace.

**Naxos' Agios Prokopios Beach: A Golden Stretch of Paradise**

Agios Prokopios Beach on the island of Naxos boasts a reputation as one of Greece's finest beaches, and it doesn't disappoint. This seemingly endless stretch of golden sands, caressed by crystal-clear waters, creates a paradise that's perfect for both relaxation and aquatic adventure.

The beach's soft sands invite visitors to spread their towels and revel in the embrace of the Mediterranean sun. The shallow, gently sloping shoreline makes it an ideal spot for families, as children can safely play in the clear and calm waters. Agios Prokopios also offers a range of water sports and activities, from kayaking and paddleboarding to windsurfing, ensuring that every kind of traveler finds their own way to enjoy the sea.

The beach is flanked by tavernas and cafes that offer delectable local cuisine, allowing visitors to savor authentic Greek flavors while gazing out over the Aegean expanse. As the sun begins to set, the sands take on a golden glow, casting a warm and magical light over the scene. Agios Prokopios Beach is not just a destination; it's a haven of relaxation and rejuvenation, where the cares of the world melt away in the embrace of sun, sand, and sea.

**Milos' Sarakiniko Beach: A Surreal Moon-Like Landscape**

Milos, a volcanic island known for its geological diversity, presents a beach unlike any other: Sarakiniko Beach. Often referred to as "lunar," this beach boasts a landscape that appears to belong to another world entirely. The juxtaposition of white volcanic rock formations against the turquoise waters of the Aegean creates a visual symphony that is as captivating as it is otherworldly.

Upon arriving at Sarakiniko Beach, visitors are greeted by a series of mesmerizing formations that look as if they were sculpted by an artist with a keen eye for the surreal. The smooth, undulating rocks resemble frozen waves or ancient sculptures, and exploring the intricate patterns and textures is an adventure in itself. The pure white of the rocks contrasts with the azure sea and sky, creating a dreamlike setting that begs for admiration and contemplation.

As the sun arcs across the sky, the changing angles of light cast shifting shadows and highlights over the rocks, revealing new facets of their beauty. It's a paradise for photographers, who can capture the interplay of light and shadow to create evocative and captivating images. The beach's popularity is a testament to its allure, drawing nature lovers, explorers, and those seeking a unique and enchanting escape.

Sarakiniko Beach is not just a beach; it's an ethereal canvas painted by the forces of nature. Its moon-like landscape and tranquil atmosphere invite visitors to step into a world that feels both timeless and mystical, a place where reality blurs and imagination takes flight.

## Scenic Hikes and Nature Trails: Exploring the Islands on Foot

For those who love to hike and immerse themselves in nature, the Cyclades offer an array of scenic trails and pathways:

### Naxos' Mount Zeus Hike: Embark on a Journey to the Highest Point in the Cyclades for Panoramic Views of the Archipelago

Naxos, the largest island in the Cyclades, beckons hikers and nature enthusiasts to undertake a remarkable journey to its pinnacle - Mount Zeus. Rising to an elevation of 1,004 meters (3,294 feet), Mount Zeus holds the distinction of being the highest peak not only on Naxos but across the entire Cycladic archipelago. The trek up this majestic mountain offers a profound connection with both nature and history, rewarding adventurers with breathtaking panoramic views that stretch across the azure Aegean Sea and the charming Cyclades islands.

## *Preparation and Starting Point*

Embarking on the Mount Zeus hike requires a degree of preparation and the right mindset. While not exceedingly challenging, the hike demands a certain level of physical fitness and a keen spirit of exploration. The ideal time to undertake this trek is during the milder months of spring or autumn when the weather is more conducive for outdoor activities. Make sure to wear comfortable hiking shoes, pack sufficient water, snacks, sunscreen, and a hat to shield yourself from the sun.

The hike typically commences from the village of Filoti, a picturesque settlement nestled in the heart of Naxos. This village serves as the gateway to the hike, offering a glimpse into the local way of life before you ascend into the heights.

## *The Ascent: A Path Through History and Nature*

The trail to Mount Zeus is a blend of history and natural beauty. As you ascend, you'll traverse ancient stone-paved paths that once connected settlements and facilitated trade among the islanders. These well-worn pathways are reminiscent of the island's historical significance and the interconnectedness of its communities.

The ascent presents a kaleidoscope of flora and fauna unique to the Cyclades. Fragrant herbs, wildflowers, and shrubs create a tapestry of colors and scents, while the distant calls of birds provide a melodic backdrop to your journey. The terrain gradually transitions from rustic paths to rocky slopes, providing a mix of challenge and wonder.

## *The Summit and Panoramic Rewards*

As you reach the summit, a triumphant sense of accomplishment washes over you. The panoramic views that unfold from this vantage point are nothing short of awe-inspiring. The expansive azure waters of the Aegean Sea stretch out in all directions, punctuated by the myriad shapes and sizes of neighboring islands. From Mykonos to Paros, and even the distant silhouette of Santorini on clear days, the Cyclades reveal their interconnectedness in a stunning display.

The summit of Mount Zeus also holds a historical significance that deepens the sense of wonder. In Greek mythology, this peak was believed to be the dwelling place of Zeus, the king of the gods. As you stand atop the highest point in the Cyclades, you can't help but feel a connection to the myths and legends that have shaped the culture of this enchanting region.

## *Descent and Reflection*

Descending from the summit allows you to savor the views from different angles and truly appreciate the island's topography. The journey down offers time for reflection, allowing you to contemplate the vastness of the Aegean expanse and the indelible mark it leaves on those fortunate enough to witness its beauty.

The Mount Zeus hike on Naxos is more than just a physical journey; it's a spiritual and emotional experience that connects you with both nature and history. It's a chance to stand at the crossroads of myth and reality, to witness the interplay of light and sea, and to embrace the essence of the Cyclades from its loftiest point.

Note: While the hike is generally accessible to most hikers, it's always advisable to check trail conditions, weather forecasts, and your own physical capabilities before attempting any hiking adventure. Respect for nature, adherence to marked paths, and responsible hiking practices are essential.

## *Sifnos' Artemonas to Apollonia Trail: Wander through Charming Villages and Scenic Landscapes as You Explore the Heart of Sifnos*

Sifnos, a gem within the Cyclades, boasts a trail that not only traverses landscapes of natural beauty but also delves into the heart of its culture and tradition. The Artemonas to Apollonia Trail offers a journey that weaves together the island's charming villages, rolling hills, and glimpses of the Aegean Sea, inviting you to discover the essence of Sifnos in a single hike.

### Beginning in Artemonas: The Town of Art and History

The trail starts in Artemonas, a village known for its quaint architecture, cobblestone alleys, and vibrant art scene. As you set out, you'll be greeted by white-washed houses adorned with colorful doors and windows, a signature of the Cycladic style. The town's rich history is evident in the preserved mansions and churches that line the streets, each revealing a piece of Sifnos' cultural tapestry.

## The Path of Olive Groves and Panoramic Views

Leaving Artemonas, the trail leads you through olive groves, offering a glimpse into the island's agricultural heritage. The scent of wild herbs fills the air as you traverse the undulating terrain, each step revealing breathtaking views of the Aegean Sea. The Cyclades archipelago emerges in the distance, a reminder of the interconnectedness of these islands.

## Charming Villages and Timeless Landscapes

As you continue, the trail takes you through the heart of Sifnos, connecting you to its villages and landscapes. Passing through Exambela, you'll be immersed in the rural simplicity of traditional island life. The trail reveals more of the island's character as you encounter terraced hillsides adorned with olive trees and vineyards. The harmony between human intervention and nature's beauty is evident in every step.

## Apollonia: The Culmination of Culture and Scenic Beauty

The trail culminates in Apollonia, Sifnos' capital and cultural hub. Apollonia is a town that effortlessly marries tradition with contemporary flair. Its narrow alleys are lined with boutiques, galleries, and cafes, inviting you to explore its creative energy. The views from Apollonia are as diverse as they are captivating, spanning both the island's interior and the coastline.

### Reflection and Connection

The Artemonas to Apollonia Trail isn't just a physical journey; it's an exploration of Sifnos' soul. The path reveals the island's history, culture, and its intrinsic connection to the land and sea. Each village you pass through, every panoramic vista you witness, adds to your understanding of Sifnos' identity.

### The Invitation to Return

As you complete the trail, a sense of fulfillment settles in. You've walked through landscapes that have witnessed generations of island life. You've wandered through villages that have preserved traditions passed down through time. And you've connected with a place that holds both its history and its future in harmony.

The Artemonas to Apollonia Trail isn't just a one-time adventure; it's an invitation to return, to discover new facets of Sifnos with each visit. It's a trail that beckons you to immerse yourself in the heart of the Cyclades, to walk in the footsteps of those who've called these islands home, and to carry the essence of Sifnos with you wherever you go.

Note: As with any outdoor activity, ensure you're adequately prepared for the trail, including wearing appropriate footwear, carrying water and snacks, and checking weather conditions. Respect for local customs, the environment, and responsible hiking practices are integral to preserving the integrity of this beautiful trail.

## Amorgos' Monastery of Panagia Hozoviotissa Trail: A Journey to a Stunning Monastery Perched on a Cliffside, Offering Breathtaking Vistas of the Aegean Sea

Amorgos, a rugged and captivating island in the Cyclades, holds a secret treasure that beckons to adventurers and seekers of beauty alike: the Monastery of Panagia Hozoviotissa. This hidden gem is not just a place of worship; it's a testament to human perseverance, devotion, and the sheer majesty of nature. The trail leading to the monastery offers a transformative journey that takes you from the coastal village of Amorgos to a breathtaking sanctuary perched on a cliffside, with the vast expanse of the Aegean Sea as your backdrop.

### *Commencing in Amorgos: A Coastal Prelude*

The trail begins in Amorgos' main village, where the sea breeze carries whispers of the Aegean and the island's maritime history. As you set off, the trail gently leads you through a landscape that reflects Amorgos' wild and rugged beauty. The path is marked by local flora and flora, painting a picture of the island's unique ecosystem.

## *Ascending the Cliffside: A Spiritual and Physical Ascent*

As you leave the village behind, the trail ascends, guiding you toward the heart of the island and the iconic Monastery of Panagia Hozoviotissa. This ascent is more than just a physical journey; it mirrors a spiritual pilgrimage, a passage of reflection and contemplation.

The pathway, etched into the rugged cliffs, grants you glimpses of the crystalline sea below. You'll find yourself pausing often, not only to catch your breath but to marvel at the sheer beauty of the landscape. The sapphire waters stretching endlessly before you are a reminder of the vastness of the world and your place within it.

## *The Monastery: A Monument of Devotion and Beauty*

As you approach the Monastery of Panagia Hozoviotissa, its presence becomes more apparent with every step. This remarkable structure, built into the cliffside with astounding precision, seems to merge seamlessly with the natural rock formations. Its whitewashed walls and blue-domed chapels are a testament to the Cycladic architectural style, and its very existence is a tribute to the island's unwavering faith.

Entering the monastery is akin to stepping into a sacred haven. Iconography, religious artifacts, and the serene atmosphere envelop you. It's a place to offer gratitude, seek solace, and marvel at the dedication of those who built this sanctuary nearly a millennium ago.

### *Panoramic Vistas and the Aegean Horizon*

As you step out onto the monastery's terrace, a breathtaking panorama unfolds before you. The vast expanse of the Aegean Sea stretches as far as the eye can see, its azure hues blending seamlessly with the sky. The wind carries the whispers of history, the stories of sailors and pilgrims who have sought refuge in this sanctuary.

From this vantage point, you're not just a visitor; you're a witness to the eternal dance of sea and sky, to the cycle of days and nights that have passed over Amorgos for centuries. It's a reminder that the human journey is but a small part of the grand tapestry of existence.

### *The Descent: Carrying the Essence of Amorgos*

As you begin your descent back to the village, the memories of the trail stay with you. The Monastery of Panagia Hozoviotissa leaves an indelible mark, not only as a physical place but as a spiritual beacon that guides your thoughts long after you've left its walls.

The Amorgos' Monastery of Panagia Hozoviotissa Trail is more than a hike; it's an immersion into the island's soul. It's a journey that connects you to the island's past, present, and future. And as you leave, you carry the essence of this experience with you, a reminder of the enduring power of faith, beauty, and the boundless expanse of the Aegean Sea.

Note: Respect for the monastery's rules and regulations, as well as responsible hiking practices, are essential. Ensure that you're properly prepared for the hike and aware of the trail's conditions. The beauty of this trail is matched only by its significance, so approach it with reverence and a sense of adventure.

## Tinos' Volax Hike: Walking through a Surreal Lunar-Like Landscape of Gigantic Boulders in a Unique and Captivating Setting

Tinos, an island known for its cultural richness and spiritual significance, also holds a geological marvel that is nothing short of mesmerizing. The Volax Hike takes you on a journey through a landscape that seems to belong to another world entirely. Imagine walking amidst colossal boulders that dot the terrain like fallen giants' playthings. This trail offers an experience that merges the otherworldly with the serene, inviting you to explore a surreal lunar-like landscape unlike anything you've encountered before.

### The Beginning: Entering the World of Giants

The trail commences in the village of Volax, where time seems to have stood still, and the air carries a sense of wonder. As you step onto the path, the enormity of the boulders begins to reveal itself. It's as if you've wandered into the remnants of a mythical battle between giants, leaving behind an awe-inspiring playground of stones.

### *Walking Amongst Giants: A Playful Landscape*

The hike takes you amidst these gigantic boulders, each one unique in its shape and form. Some stand as solitary sentinels, while others cluster together like nature's own puzzle pieces. The path winds its way through this geological wonderland, creating an experience that feels both humbling and enchanting.

As you navigate the trail, your imagination might conjure stories of ancient gods and heroes playing games with these massive stones. The formations seem to invite you to explore their crevices, to marvel at their intricacies, and to wonder at the forces that shaped them over millennia.

### *A Glimpse into Geology: Forces of Nature*

The boulders that define the Volax landscape are not merely random formations; they're the result of complex geological processes that have unfolded over eons. The island's volcanic origins and the forces of erosion have sculpted this lunar-like terrain, creating a geological masterpiece that is as educational as it is visually stunning.

### *The Silence of Surreality: Moments of Reflection*

Amidst the silence of this unique landscape, there's a certain meditative quality to the hike. The sense of being in a place that is both familiar and foreign prompts introspection. As you walk amongst the boulders, you're offered a moment to connect with the raw power of nature, to contemplate the passage of time, and to marvel at the universe's capacity for diversity and creation.

## *Captivating Sights: A Journey of Uniqueness*

As you continue your hike, the uniqueness of Volax continues to unfold. The boulders reveal hidden nooks, providing shelter for plants that thrive in this unconventional environment. The contrast between the rugged stones and the delicate flora creates a visual poetry that adds to the allure of the landscape.

## *Returning with Memories and Reflections*

Completing the Volax Hike isn't just about reaching the end of the trail; it's about leaving with a collection of memories and reflections. The lunar-like landscape, the whispers of the wind as it dances through the stones, and the sheer surrealism of the experience become a part of you. It's a journey that challenges your perception of the world and leaves you with a sense of reverence for the forces that shape our planet.

The Volax Hike on Tinos is more than a hike; it's a voyage to a land of giants, a glimpse into the Earth's creative processes, and an opportunity to connect with the marvels of nature. It's a reminder that even in the most unexpected corners of the world, beauty and wonder await those willing to explore.

Note: As with any outdoor adventure, ensure you're well-prepared for the trail, including wearing appropriate footwear and carrying water and necessary supplies. Respect for the environment and responsible hiking practices are essential to preserve the integrity of this unique landscape.

## Water Sports and Marine Adventures: Diving, Snorkeling, and more

The crystal-clear waters surrounding the Cyclades provide the perfect playground for water enthusiasts:

### *Snorkeling in Antiparos' Blue Cave: Dive into the Mesmerizing Blue Waters of this Cave, Where Sunlight Creates a Surreal Underwater World*

Nestled within the embrace of the Cyclades archipelago, the island of Antiparos holds a hidden gem that captivates the hearts of snorkelers and adventurers alike—the enchanting Blue Cave. This natural wonder is a testament to the magic that nature can conjure, as it beckons visitors to explore its otherworldly beauty beneath the surface.

#### *Discovering the Blue Cave's Entrance*

Accessible by boat from the main harbor of Antiparos, the journey to the Blue Cave is an adventure in itself. As you glide across the crystalline waters of the Aegean Sea, the sight of the cave's entrance gradually comes into view, an inviting opening carved into the rocky coastline. The entrance's arched silhouette stands in stark contrast to the azure sea, hinting at the ethereal experience that lies beyond.

## *Entering the Realm of Azure*

Stepping into a small boat, your anticipation grows as you approach the cave's entrance. Once inside, the transformation is instantaneous. The sunlight filtering through the water casts an enchanting blue hue, reflecting off the cave's limestone walls and creating a mesmerizing, almost dreamlike, environment. The sensation of stepping into another world is palpable—a sensation shared by explorers for generations.

## *Underwater Serenity and Marine Life*

Slipping into the cool embrace of the Aegean waters, you're immediately greeted by a tranquil underwater scene. The cave's interior opens up, revealing an expanse of azure brilliance. The clarity of the water allows for exceptional visibility, granting you the privilege of observing the marine life that calls this unique environment home.

Schools of colorful fish dart in and out of the recesses, their vibrant hues contrasting beautifully against the cave's cerulean backdrop. Delicate sea anemones sway with the gentle currents, and if you're fortunate, you might catch a glimpse of a curious octopus camouflaged among the rocks.

### *Sunlit Reflections and Otherworldly Moments*

As you venture deeper into the cave, you'll notice how the play of light takes center stage. Sunlight pierces through the water's surface, creating ethereal beams that dance and shimmer around you. The water's surface seems to come alive with reflections, casting intricate patterns on the cave walls and seafloor below.

In some areas, the cave's ceiling is adorned with formations that seem almost celestial, resembling stars in a night sky. These formations, sculpted by time and water, add to the mystical ambiance of the environment. Floating amidst this symphony of light and shadow, you'll find yourself lost in a world of otherworldly beauty that few have the chance to witness.

### *The Journey's End and Lasting Impressions*

As you reluctantly ascend to the water's surface, the memory of your underwater exploration lingers like a dream. The Blue Cave of Antiparos leaves an indelible mark on those fortunate enough to experience its enchantment. This natural wonder is a testament to the beauty of our world—a reminder that beneath the surface of even the most unassuming locations, there can be hidden pockets of magic waiting to be discovered.

## *Wind and Kite Surfing in Paros: Take Advantage of the Cyclades' Famed Winds to Indulge in Thrilling Water Sports off Paros' Coasts*

The Cyclades islands are famed for their stunning landscapes, azure waters, and consistent winds—qualities that have made Paros a haven for wind and kite surfers from around the world. With its idyllic beaches, reliable wind patterns, and vibrant water sports community, Paros offers the perfect playground for those seeking the adrenaline rush of wind and kite surfing.

### The Windswept Paradise of Paros

Paros, often referred to as the "kiteboarding capital of Greece," boasts a natural setting that is tailor-made for wind and kite surfing enthusiasts. Its gently curving bays and clear waters are complemented by the Meltemi winds that sweep across the Cyclades during the summer months. These winds create the ideal conditions for both beginners looking to learn the sport and experienced surfers craving a challenge.

### Harnessing the Power of the Wind

Wind and kite surfing involve the exhilarating experience of riding the waves while being propelled by the force of the wind. In Paros, the Meltemi winds provide a reliable and consistent source of energy, ensuring that surfers can enjoy hours of uninterrupted excitement. The island's various beaches offer a range of conditions suited to different skill levels, making it an inclusive destination for surfers of all proficiency levels.

### *Kite Surfing: A Dance with the Elements*

Kite surfing, a fusion of wakeboarding, windsurfing, and paragliding, takes the water sports experience to new heights. The vibrant kites, with their colorful sails, add a touch of spectacle to the serene seascape. As a kite surfer, you'll feel the exhilaration of being suspended between the sky and the sea, your kite responding to the tug of the wind as you glide gracefully across the water's surface.

### *Wind Surfing: Embracing the Elements*

For those who prefer the classic thrill of windsurfing, Paros provides a playground for mastering the art of riding the waves with a sail and board. The combination of wind, water, and balance creates an exciting synergy, allowing windsurfers to feel a profound connection with the elements. The sense of accomplishment as you navigate the waves and catch the wind is second to none.

### *Learning and Advancing*

Paros is home to a variety of wind and kite surfing schools and rental shops that cater to beginners and veterans alike. If you're new to the sport, you'll find patient instructors ready to guide you through the basics, from controlling the kite to standing on the board. For more experienced surfers, Paros offers the opportunity to refine your skills and tackle more challenging conditions.

### Community and Camaraderie

Beyond the adrenaline rush, wind and kite surfing in Paros offers a chance to connect with like-minded individuals who share your passion for the water and the wind. The island's water sports community is welcoming and diverse, creating an atmosphere of camaraderie that extends from the beach to the local cafes and hangouts.

### Embrace the Adventure

Wind and kite surfing in Paros is more than just a sport—it's an adventure that allows you to embrace the elements, challenge yourself, and revel in the exhilaration of harnessing the power of wind and water. Whether you're a seasoned surfer or a newcomer to the scene, Paros invites you to ride the waves, feel the wind in your sails, and experience the thrill of this dynamic water sport in one of the world's most stunning settings.

## Scuba Diving in Mykonos: Explore Vibrant Marine Life, Ancient Shipwrecks, and Underwater Caves in the Depths of the Aegean Sea

The allure of Mykonos extends far beyond its vibrant nightlife and picturesque white-washed buildings. Beneath the surface of the azure Aegean Sea lies an underwater world waiting to be explored—rich in history, teeming with marine life, and filled with the intrigue of sunken shipwrecks and hidden caves. Scuba diving in Mykonos offers a unique perspective of this iconic Cycladic island.

### Diving into Mykonos' Underwater Realm

Mykonos' underwater landscape is a testament to the island's storied history and diverse marine ecosystems. Whether you're a seasoned diver or a newcomer to the world of scuba, the island's dive sites offer an array of experiences to suit every skill level and interest.

### Vibrant Marine Life

Submerging beneath the surface, you'll encounter a kaleidoscope of marine life that populates the Aegean waters. Schools of colorful fish, from damselfish to wrasses, weave intricate patterns through the clear blue expanse. Sea fans and sponges adorn the rocky formations, creating a habitat that supports a myriad of species.

### Exploring Ancient Shipwrecks

One of the highlights of diving in Mykonos is the opportunity to explore ancient shipwrecks that have found their resting place on the seabed. These underwater time capsules offer a glimpse into history, transporting divers back in time to eras when these vessels sailed the Aegean waters. As you swim among the timeworn remains, you can't help but feel a sense of awe and reverence for the stories these wrecks hold.

## *Unveiling Underwater Caves and Grottoes*

Mykonos' underwater terrain is marked by captivating underwater caves and grottoes, each with its own unique character. These submerged chambers are often adorned with intricate rock formations and are inhabited by a diverse array of marine life. Exploring these hidden realms is akin to embarking on an underwater treasure hunt—a journey that rewards the intrepid diver with moments of wonder and discovery.

## *Preparation and Dive Centers*

For those eager to experience the underwater wonders of Mykonos, the island boasts several reputable dive centers that cater to divers of all experience levels. Whether you're a beginner seeking guidance or a certified diver looking for a new adventure, these centers offer a range of services, from introductory courses to guided dive excursions.

## *Diving Ethics and Conservation*

As you explore the depths of the Aegean Sea, it's crucial to approach your underwater adventures with a sense of responsibility and conservation. Mykonos' dive centers prioritize sustainable diving practices, ensuring that the marine ecosystems remain unspoiled for generations to come. Adhering to diving ethics and respecting the underwater environment is an essential part of the diving experience in Mykonos.

### The Adventure Continues

Scuba diving in Mykonos is more than a recreational activity—it's an immersion into a world that exists beneath the waves, a realm of history, life, and beauty that exists in tandem with the island's more well-known attractions. As you explore the underwater landscapes, you'll come to appreciate the dynamic interplay between the island's terrestrial and aquatic realms, ultimately forging a deeper connection with this captivating Cycladic destination.

## Connecting with the Past: Archaeological Sites and Historical Tours

Immerse yourself in the rich history and cultural heritage of the Cyclades by visiting ancient sites and partaking in historical tours:

### Delos: The UNESCO World Heritage Site

Nestled in the heart of the Aegean Sea, the small island of Delos stands as a testament to both ancient mythology and historical significance. Renowned as the mythological birthplace of Apollo and Artemis, the island's rich history and archeological wonders have earned it the prestigious title of a UNESCO World Heritage Site.

## Myth and History Intertwined

According to ancient Greek mythology, Leto, the mother of Apollo and Artemis, sought refuge on Delos to escape the wrath of Hera. It is said that Leto gave birth to her divine twins on this sacred land, thus establishing Delos as a hub of mythological significance. Over time, the island became a major religious and cultural center, attracting pilgrims and visitors from across the Greek world.

## A Glimpse into Delos' Archeological Marvels

Today, Delos offers modern-day explorers a unique opportunity to step back in time and witness the remnants of its ancient glory. As you set foot on the island, you're transported to an era when Delos flourished as a bustling trade hub and religious center.

The Sanctuary of Apollo: One of the most iconic features of Delos is the Sanctuary of Apollo, a sprawling complex dedicated to the god of music, prophecy, and healing. The centerpiece of the sanctuary is the Terrace of the Lions, a row of marble lion statues that stand as silent guardians, each embodying its own unique charm and expression.

The Avenue of the Lions: This awe-inspiring pathway leads from the harbor to the Sanctuary of Apollo. The avenue is lined with the famous marble lions, sculpted in various poses, some reclining and others in a seated position. These intricate sculptures not only showcase the mastery of ancient Greek art but also symbolize the island's reverence for Apollo.

Well-Preserved Mosaics and Residences: As you wander through the ancient streets, you'll encounter well-preserved mosaics and the remains of grand residences. These homes provide insights into the daily lives of the island's inhabitants, showcasing their appreciation for art, culture, and luxury.

## Akrotiri Archaeological Site in Santorini

Venture to the mesmerizing island of Santorini, known for its breathtaking sunsets and dramatic landscapes, and you'll have the chance to uncover an ancient secret buried beneath layers of volcanic ash.

### The Ancient Minoan City

Akrotiri, located on the southern end of Santorini, offers a window into the world of the Minoans, one of the most advanced civilizations of the ancient world. The city was a thriving settlement in the Bronze Age, with evidence of sophisticated urban planning, multi-story buildings, and advanced drainage systems.

### Preserved by Catastrophe

Around 1600 BC, a catastrophic volcanic eruption buried the city under layers of ash and pumice, preserving it remarkably well over the millennia. As a result, Akrotiri is often referred to as the "Pompeii of the Aegean," providing archeologists and historians with invaluable insights into prehistoric life.

### Unveiling Prehistoric Life

Upon exploring the archaeological site, you'll encounter streets, buildings, and even furniture that paint a vivid picture of daily life in Akrotiri. Elaborate frescoes depicting nature, animals, and daily activities adorn the walls, providing a glimpse into the artistic sensibilities of the Minoans.

## Paros' Valley of the Butterflies

For a different kind of historical and natural spectacle, journey to Paros and discover the enchanting Valley of the Butterflies.

### A Haven for Butterflies

Nestled in the heart of Paros, the Valley of the Butterflies is a lush, serene haven that attracts thousands of Jersey tiger moths during their annual migration. The spectacle begins around June and lasts until September, as the trees and streams of the valley become a temporary home for these delicate creatures.

### Walking through a Butterfly Symphony

As you stroll along the designated pathways, you'll find yourself enveloped in a magical world. The vibrant fluttering of countless butterflies creates a symphony of color and movement, making it seem as if you've stepped into a living canvas.

## Preservation Efforts

Efforts have been made to maintain the natural habitat of the butterflies and minimize human impact. Wooden bridges and pathways allow visitors to explore the valley without disturbing its delicate ecosystem.

From the mythical aura of Delos to the buried history of Akrotiri and the delicate dance of butterflies in Paros, the Cyclades islands offer an array of activities that cater to both history enthusiasts and nature lovers alike. These sites stand as bridges between ancient civilizations and the modern world, reminding us of the intricate tapestry of human and natural history that weaves through the Aegean archipelago.
Engaging in these activities and adventures will not only allow you to experience the beauty and diversity of the Cyclades but also create memories that will last a lifetime.

# Chapter 6: Travel Itineraries

## Family-Friendly Itineraries in the Cyclades: Crafting Unforgettable Adventures for All Ages

Traveling with the family is a cherished experience, and the Cyclades archipelago offers an idyllic backdrop for creating lifelong memories together. From the captivating beaches and charming villages to interactive cultural encounters and outdoor activities, the Cyclades cater to every member of the family. In this section, we'll delve into comprehensive family-friendly itineraries across various islands, ensuring that every day is filled with wonder and delight.

### Day 1: Arrival in Santorini

Your family's Cyclades adventure begins as you touch down on the captivating island of Santorini. The moment you step off the plane or ferry, you're welcomed by the island's enchanting aura. After a smooth arrival and perhaps a short transfer, you settle into your carefully chosen family-friendly accommodation, ensuring comfort and convenience for all members, young and old.

Once you've settled in, it's time to venture into the heart of the Cyclades gem. Your first stop is the picturesque town of

Fira. As you wind through its labyrinthine streets, the iconic architecture of whitewashed buildings and blue domes transports you to a world of postcard-perfect beauty. The charming cobblestone streets invite you for an evening stroll, where each corner reveals another picturesque scene to capture your family's imagination.

A notable highlight of your first day is the Museum of Prehistoric Thira, an engaging destination for both children and adults. This museum offers a journey back in time, sharing the island's rich history through a collection of captivating artifacts. It's a fantastic opportunity to introduce your children to the mysteries of ancient civilizations and spark their curiosity about the past.

As the sun begins to set over the azure sea, head to Fira's lookout points to savor the panoramic view of the caldera. This awe-inspiring sight is a true marvel of nature, and it's an experience that will undoubtedly captivate every member of the family. As you soak in the golden hues of the setting sun, you're setting the tone for a week of unforgettable memories.

**Day 2: Santorini's Coastal Wonders**

Awake to the gentle breeze and the anticipation of another incredible day in the Cyclades. Today, you're embracing the coastline, and your first stop is Kamari Beach. This renowned black sand beach offers a unique setting for family fun. The smooth sands and shallow, gentle waters provide an ideal playground for kids. As they build sandcastles and play beach volleyball, you can lounge under the sun, knowing that your little ones are safe and having a blast.

A picnic on the beach is a delightful way to refuel and spend quality time together. Savor local delicacies as you enjoy the laid-back atmosphere and stunning views that Kamari Beach offers. The Aegean Sea stretches before you, inviting you to dive in and cool off whenever the mood strikes.

In the afternoon, an adventure awaits as you embark on a boat trip to the volcanic islets of Nea Kameni and Palea Kameni. This expedition offers a fascinating blend of education and exploration for the whole family. As you arrive at Nea Kameni, your family can embark on a moderate hike to the rim of an active volcano. It's a thrilling experience to stand on the edge of this natural wonder and gaze into its depths.

After the hike, the adventure continues as you visit Palea Kameni's therapeutic hot springs. The family can take a dip in these warm waters, which are believed to have healing properties. It's a unique experience that combines relaxation and excitement – a perfect way to bond as a family.

As the day winds down, you'll return to Santorini's shores with a sense of accomplishment and an appreciation for the island's geological wonders.

**Day 3: Mykonos' Family Delights**

Today, you bid farewell to Santorini and board a ferry or flight to the vibrant island of Mykonos. Known for its lively atmosphere and family-friendly charm, Mykonos promises a day of delightful exploration.

Your first stop is Mykonos Town, a maze of narrow streets that wind through whitewashed buildings adorned with colorful doors and windows. This labyrinthine layout is a delight for kids and adults alike, offering a sense of adventure as you explore the enchanting alleyways. Allow your children's curiosity to lead the way, as you uncover hidden boutiques, quaint cafes, and charming squares.

A highlight for cultural enrichment is a visit to the Mykonos Folklore Museum. This engaging institution provides an opportunity for your children to connect with the island's past. Through traditional costumes, artifacts, and exhibits, they'll gain insight into Mykonos' history and traditions, fostering an appreciation for local culture.

After your cultural exploration, it's time to embrace the sun and sea. Head to Ornos Beach, known for its calm waters and family-friendly amenities. While the kids engage in water sports or build sandcastles, you can relax under the shade of an umbrella, basking in the beauty of the Aegean. Ornos Beach offers a safe and welcoming environment for families, ensuring everyone can enjoy the water at their own pace.

As the day transitions into evening, savor a traditional Greek dinner at a seaside taverna. Let the flavors of Greek cuisine delight your taste buds as you enjoy the company of your loved ones against the backdrop of the setting sun over the sparkling sea.

## Day 4: Island Exploration in Naxos

Wake up to the anticipation of discovering another Cycladic gem – Naxos. Known for its laid-back atmosphere and family-friendly offerings, Naxos is a haven for families seeking both relaxation and adventure.

Your first stop is Naxos Town, where the Venetian castle offers a glimpse into the island's history. Here, you'll find the Portara, a massive marble doorway that stands as a symbol of Naxos' ancient glory. As you explore the castle grounds, your children can imagine life in a time long past.

Later, head to Agios Georgios Beach, a haven of gentle waves and golden sands. This family-friendly beach is ideal for both splashing in the water and building sandcastles. Allow your children to engage in imaginative play while you relax under the sun, enjoying the simple pleasures of island life.

To add an extra layer of adventure, consider renting bicycles for the family. Naxos' landscape is dotted with quaint villages and picturesque landscapes, making it a cyclist's paradise. Ride through charming villages, passing by vineyards and olive groves, and stop for lunch at a local taverna to savor authentic Greek flavors.

As the sun sets on your day of exploration, you'll realize that Naxos has captured your family's hearts with its serene beauty and welcoming atmosphere.

## Day 5: Active Adventures in Paros

Embrace the spirit of adventure as you set foot on Paros, an island that offers a perfect blend of outdoor activities and family-friendly attractions.

Your day begins with an invigorating hike through the Paros Park trails. This natural reserve boasts a network of paths that lead to stunning viewpoints and secluded beaches. The whole family can engage in this active exploration, with each step revealing a new facet of Paros' natural beauty. The breathtaking vistas and fresh sea breezes make this experience truly unforgettable.

As you descend from your hike, it's time for a leisurely afternoon at Kolymbithres Beach. This unique beach is characterized by its fascinating rock formations that provide natural shade and shelter. The calm waters are ideal for kids to safely swim and play, while you can relax on the beach and enjoy the surroundings. Encourage your children's curiosity by exploring the intriguing rock formations and perhaps finding a hidden treasure within the rocks.

For an interactive experience that also channels the island's artistic spirit, engage in a pottery workshop in the charming village of Naoussa. This hands-on activity allows your children to tap into their creativity and create their own ceramic masterpieces under the guidance of local artisans. It's a fantastic opportunity to connect with the island's culture and bring home a tangible memory of your time in Paros.

As the day draws to a close, you'll find that Paros has offered your family a balanced combination of active adventure and cultural engagement, leaving you with a sense of satisfaction and excitement for the days ahead.

**Day 6: Cultural Exploration in Tinos**

Ferry to Tinos, an island renowned for its religious significance and artistic heritage. Today's itinerary offers a blend of spiritual exploration and relaxation by the sea.

Begin your day by exploring the picturesque village of Pyrgos, where traditional marble craftsmen continue to shape the island's artistic identity. Witness the intricate process of marble carving and discover how this material has played a central role in Tinos' culture for generations. Allow your children to interact with the craftsmen and gain a deeper appreciation for this timeless art form.

As you continue your cultural exploration, visit the Church of Panagia Evangelistria in Tinos Town. This pilgrimage site holds great significance for locals and visitors alike. Share the island's spiritual side with your children and encourage them to ask questions about faith and culture, fostering an open dialogue and understanding.

Spend your afternoon at Agios Fokas Beach, where shallow, calm waters and soft sands create the perfect environment for family relaxation. Allow your children to explore the shoreline, collect seashells, and perhaps even engage in a friendly game of beach volleyball. As you soak in the sun and sea, you'll find that Tinos offers a serene and reflective atmosphere that complements your family's journey.

## Day 7: Beach Bliss and Farewell in Milos

As your Cyclades adventure nears its end, there's no better place to conclude your journey than on the enchanting island of Milos.

Today, you're in for a treat as you visit Sarakiniko Beach, a place of otherworldly beauty. The surreal white rock formations against the backdrop of the clear blue waters create a dreamlike atmosphere that appeals to the imagination of both children and adults. Spend your morning here, exploring the unique landscape, wading in the shallow waters, and capturing the essence of this breathtaking beach.

In the afternoon, prepare for a family-friendly snorkeling excursion to Kleftiko. This remote cove is a hidden gem with sea caves, crystal-clear waters, and an underwater world waiting to be discovered. Don your snorkeling gear and dive into a realm of vibrant marine life and hidden wonders. This experience is not only fun and engaging but also educational as your children gain insights into the marine ecosystem.

As the sun begins to set on your final day in the Cyclades, find a comfortable spot to enjoy a sunset picnic overlooking the sea. Reflect on the incredible journey you've shared as a family – the moments of discovery, the laughter, and the bonds strengthened along the way. The beauty of the Cyclades has served as a backdrop for your family's unforgettable adventure, leaving you with memories to treasure for a lifetime.

Conclusion

Your family-friendly itinerary through the Cyclades has provided a harmonious blend of exploration, relaxation, cultural engagement, and outdoor adventures. Each day has been meticulously crafted to cater to the interests and needs of every member of the family, ensuring that each moment is cherished and every experience shared.

As you bid farewell to the Cyclades, you'll carry with you a sense of fulfillment, a deeper connection with your loved ones, and a newfound appreciation for the beauty and diversity that this stunning archipelago offers. Your family's adventure in the Cyclades will forever remain a chapter of shared joy, discovery, and growth.

# 5-Day Travel Itineraries for Exploring the Cyclades

When planning a journey to the Cyclades, a captivating archipelago in the Aegean Sea, crafting a well-structured itinerary is key to making the most of your experience. With a rich tapestry of islands, each offering its own distinct allure, it's essential to strike a balance between exploration, relaxation, and cultural immersion. Here, we present two diverse 5-day travel itineraries, each tailored to offer a unique encounter with the Cyclades' beauty and charm.

# Itinerary 1: Island-Hopping Extravaganza

Day 1: Arrival in Mykonos

- Morning: Arrive in Mykonos, often dubbed the "Island of the Winds." Stroll through the charming streets of Mykonos Town (Chora), characterized by its whitewashed buildings and iconic windmills.
- Afternoon: Relax at Agios Ioannis Beach, renowned for its crystal-clear waters and stunning sunset views.
- Evening: Enjoy Mykonos' vibrant nightlife and dine at a seaside taverna.

Day 2: Delos Exploration

- Morning: Embark on a boat tour to the sacred island of Delos, an archaeological treasure trove. Explore ancient ruins, temples, and mosaics that showcase the island's significance in Greek mythology.
- Afternoon: Return to Mykonos and spend your afternoon at Paradise Beach, known for its lively atmosphere and beach parties.
- Evening: Savor fresh seafood at a waterfront restaurant.

Day 3: Naxos Adventure

- Morning: Take a ferry to Naxos, the largest island in the Cyclades. Visit Naxos Town and explore the historic Kastro district.

- Afternoon: Relax on Agios Georgios Beach or engage in water sports.
- Evening: Dine in the charming alleys of Naxos Town and experience the island's vibrant nightlife.

Day 4: Beach Bliss in Paros

- Morning: Ferry to Paros and visit Parikia, the island's capital. Explore the Ekatontapyliani Church, a Byzantine jewel.
- Afternoon: Discover Kolymbithres Beach with its unique rock formations and natural pools.
- Evening: Head to Naoussa, a picturesque fishing village, for dinner at a traditional taverna.

Day 5: Farewell to the Cyclades

- Morning: Take a morning stroll on Pounda Beach and enjoy your last moments in Paros.
- Afternoon: Return to Athens via ferry or flight, cherishing memories of your Cyclades adventure.

## Itinerary 2: Serene Retreat and Cultural Delights

Day 1: Arrival in Santorini

- Morning: Arrive in Santorini and settle into your accommodation in Fira or Oia.

- Afternoon: Explore Fira's narrow streets and enjoy stunning caldera views.
- Evening: Witness a legendary Santorini sunset from Oia's cliffs.

Day 2: Exploring Santorini's Mystique

- Morning: Visit the ancient site of Akrotiri, a well-preserved Minoan city.
- Afternoon: Relax at Perissa Black Sand Beach or the Red Beach.
- Evening: Savor a candlelit dinner with volcanic vistas.

Day 3: Tranquility in Folegandros

- Morning: Ferry to Folegandros, an off-the-beaten-path gem.
- Afternoon: Stroll through the charming town of Chora and admire its Cycladic architecture.
- Evening: Enjoy a leisurely dinner at a local taverna.

Day 4: Immersion in Milos' Diversity

- Morning: Ferry to Milos, known for its diverse landscapes.
- Afternoon: Discover Sarakiniko Beach's unique lunar landscape and swim in its turquoise waters.
- Evening: Dine in the picturesque village of Plaka.

Day 5: Goodbye, Cyclades

- Morning: Visit the ancient theater of Milos before departing.
- Afternoon: Return to Athens, reflecting on your enriching Cyclades journey.

These itineraries offer a glimpse into the rich variety of experiences the Cyclades have to offer. While they provide a structured framework, be sure to leave room for spontaneity and exploration, as the Cyclades have a way of surprising you with unexpected beauty and encounters.

## 7-Day Travel Itineraries for Exploring the Cyclades: Island-Hopping Adventures

The Cyclades, with their breathtaking landscapes, rich history, and vibrant culture, offer an enticing playground for travelers seeking a week-long island-hopping adventure. With a myriad of options to choose from, crafting the perfect 7-day itinerary requires thoughtful planning to ensure you make the most of your time in this stunning Greek archipelago. Here are three diverse itineraries that cater to different interests, allowing you to immerse yourself in the beauty and charm of the Cyclades.

# Itinerary 1: Beach Bliss and Relaxation

## Day 1: Arrival in Mykonos

As you step onto the shores of Mykonos, the Cyclades embrace you with its iconic energetic ambiance and awe-inspiring vistas. Known as the jewel of the Aegean, Mykonos introduces you to a world of white-washed buildings, azure waters, and a lively atmosphere that promises a captivating week ahead.

Arriving at the island's port, you're greeted by the refreshing sea breeze and the anticipation of the adventures that await. The moment you set foot on the island, you're immersed in the island's unique blend of cosmopolitan charm and traditional Greek culture.

Explore Mykonos Town (Chora)

Venture into Mykonos Town, often referred to as Chora, where you'll find a labyrinth of narrow alleys, adorned with vibrant bougainvillaea and charming shops. Wander through the maze-like streets, discovering boutiques, art galleries, and quaint cafes. The town's Cycladic architecture, with its white facades and blue accents, creates an enchanting backdrop for your exploration.

Stroll Through Charming Alleys and Enjoy a Traditional Greek Dinner

Allow the town to guide you through its intricate network of alleys, unveiling hidden courtyards and panoramic viewpoints. The iconic whitewashed buildings stand in stark contrast to the cerulean sky, creating a picture-perfect setting for every corner you turn.

As the sun begins to set, make your way to a seaside taverna for a quintessential Greek dinner. Sample local delicacies, from freshly caught seafood to mouthwatering moussaka, while you're serenaded by the lapping waves and the melodies of bouzouki music in the background.

**Day 2: Mykonos Exploration**

Relax on Paradise Beach or Super Paradise Beach

Welcome your second day with the prospect of pure relaxation on the renowned beaches of Mykonos. Choose between Paradise Beach and Super Paradise Beach, both known for their vibrant beach clubs, inviting sunbeds, and crystal-clear waters. Immerse yourself in the lively atmosphere, where DJs spin tunes and beach parties create an unparalleled energy.

Visit the Iconic Windmills and Explore Delos on a Day Trip

After a morning of seaside serenity, venture to the iconic Mykonos windmills, a symbol of the island's charm. Perched atop a hill overlooking the town, these windmills offer breathtaking panoramic views of Chora and the sea beyond.

In the afternoon, embark on a day trip to the nearby island of Delos. An archaeological treasure trove, Delos unveils ancient ruins, temples, and statues that transport you back to the days of Greek mythology. Explore the Terrace of Lions, the House of Dionysus, and the Archaeological Museum, absorbing the historical significance of this UNESCO World Heritage Site.

**Day 3: Paros Delights**

Ferry to Paros

Bid farewell to Mykonos as you board a ferry that carries you towards the picturesque island of Paros. Known for its serene beauty and authentic Greek lifestyle, Paros promises a different kind of Cycladic experience.

Discover the Old Town of Parikia and Panagia Ekatontapiliani

Upon arrival in Parikia, Paros' main port, you'll be greeted by the town's charming streets and welcoming atmosphere. Navigate the narrow pathways that lead to the heart of the old town. Here, you'll find the Panagia Ekatontapiliani, a Byzantine church with a rich history and unique architecture. Marvel at its intricate design and absorb the spiritual ambiance that surrounds it.

Soak in the Local Atmosphere

As the day unfolds, take leisurely walks along the waterfront, enjoying the views of the sea and the distant mountains.

Engage with the friendly locals, savor traditional Greek pastries at local bakeries, and let the unhurried pace of Paros ease you into its rhythm.

## Day 4: Beaches and Sunsets in Paros

Spend the Day at Kolymbithres Beach

Wake up to a day dedicated to the exploration of Paros' pristine beaches. Kolymbithres Beach, nestled among granite rock formations, promises a unique and tranquil experience. Relax on sunbeds or lay down your towel on the golden sand. The natural rock formations create natural pools, adding an element of intrigue to your beach escapade.

Head to Naoussa for Dinner and Sunset

As the sun begins to set, make your way to the charming fishing village of Naoussa. Meander through the picturesque alleys, lined with whitewashed buildings adorned with colorful flowers. Enjoy a delightful dinner at a waterfront taverna, indulging in fresh seafood and local wine as the sun dips below the horizon, casting a warm golden glow over the tranquil harbor.

## Day 5: Naxos Adventure

Ferry to Naxos

With the sun rising on your fifth day, embark on a ferry journey to Naxos, the largest island in the Cyclades. Naxos promises a blend of captivating history, diverse landscapes, and warm island hospitality.

Explore Naxos Town and Visit the Portara

Arriving in Naxos Town, you're greeted by the imposing Portara, an ancient marble gate that stands as a reminder of an unfinished temple dedicated to Apollo. As you explore Naxos Town, you'll encounter a mix of Venetian architecture and traditional Cycladic design, creating a unique visual tapestry.

Sample Local Cuisine at a Waterfront Taverna

As the sun reaches its zenith, indulge in a leisurely waterfront lunch. Savor the island's culinary delights, from freshly caught seafood to creamy tzatziki. Allow the flavors to transport you to the heart of Cycladic culture as you enjoy a meal with a view of the Aegean Sea.

**Day 6: Naxos Exploration**

Hike up to Mount Zeus

Today, embark on a hiking adventure to the summit of Mount Zeus, the highest point in the Cyclades. The trail takes you through scenic landscapes, passing by ancient olive groves and fragrant herbs. As you ascend, the panoramic views gradually unfold, rewarding your efforts with breathtaking vistas of Naxos and the surrounding archipelago.

Relax on Agios Prokopios Beach or Agia Anna Beach

In the afternoon, treat yourself to relaxation on the island's renowned beaches. Agios Prokopios Beach and Agia Anna Beach beckon with their inviting shores and crystal-clear waters. Whether you choose to unwind with a book, take a refreshing swim, or simply bask in the sun, these beaches offer a serene retreat from the world.

**Day 7: Farewell to Cyclades**

Take a Leisurely Morning Swim

As your final day in the Cyclades dawns, seize the opportunity for a leisurely morning swim in the tranquil waters of Naxos. Allow the Aegean Sea to embrace you one last time, leaving you with a sense of renewal and connection to the natural beauty that surrounds you.

Return to Athens

Bid a fond farewell to Naxos as you board your ferry or flight back to Athens. As the Cyclades recede into the distance, carry with you the memories of sun-soaked beaches, cultural discoveries, and the tranquility that defines the essence of this enchanting Greek archipelago. Until you return, let the spirit of the Cyclades remain alive in your heart, a timeless reminder of the beauty and wonder that awaits within its shores.

# Itinerary 2: Cultural Immersion and History

Day 1: Arrival in Santorini

As you step onto the shores of Santorini, the spellbinding beauty of this Aegean gem immediately envelops you. Renowned for its iconic caldera views and picturesque landscapes, Santorini sets the stage for an unforgettable adventure.

Your first destination is Fira, the island's bustling capital perched on the caldera's edge. Wind your way through its charming alleys, where whitewashed buildings contrast against the deep blue sea. As you explore, don't miss the opportunity to immerse yourself in local culture – browse boutique shops, sample traditional delicacies, and interact with the friendly locals.

As the day draws to a close, the magic of Santorini truly reveals itself during sunset at Oia. Make your way to this enchanting village that graces countless postcards and travel brochures. The sun's golden hues paint the sky as it sinks behind the horizon, casting a warm glow over the caldera and illuminating the blue-domed churches. The sight is nothing short of mesmerizing, earning Oia its reputation as one of the world's most famous sunset spots.

Day 2: Exploring Santorini's Heritage

Today's journey takes you back in time as you venture to Akrotiri, an ancient Minoan settlement preserved for millennia beneath layers of volcanic ash. Walk through the archaeological site, where you can trace the remnants of a once-thriving civilization. Intricately preserved frescoes and structures provide glimpses into the daily life of the Minoans, offering a fascinating window into history.

In the afternoon, ascend to the heights of ancient Thera, a historical marvel perched atop a mountain. The panoramic views from this vantage point are breathtaking, encompassing the azure waters of the Aegean and the rolling landscapes of Santorini. This trip through time will leave you in awe of the island's rich history and the resilience of its past inhabitants.

Day 3: Off to Crete

Embark on a ferry to Crete, the largest of the Greek islands, for an immersive day trip. Upon arrival in Heraklion, you'll be greeted by the bustling energy of the island's capital. Dive into history at the renowned archaeological site of Knossos, the legendary palace of King Minos and the center of Minoan civilization. Wander through the ruins, where storied tales of the Minotaur and the Labyrinth come to life amidst the stone walls.

Day 4: Return to Santorini

Back in Santorini, embrace the island's diversity as you unwind on Kamari Beach. The striking contrast of the volcanic black sands against the clear waters creates a unique backdrop for relaxation. Bask in the Mediterranean sun, take refreshing dips in the sea, and let the soothing sounds of the waves wash over you.

As the evening approaches, indulge in a culinary adventure. Delight your taste buds with a seafood feast by the sea, savoring the island's culinary gems. Freshly caught seafood, locally sourced ingredients, and traditional recipes combine to create a gastronomic experience that perfectly complements your day of beachside relaxation.

Day 5: Charming Folegandros

Set sail to Folegandros, a hidden treasure in the Cyclades that invites you to step into a world of timeless charm. As you arrive, the quaint simplicity of the island's landscapes and architecture captivates your senses. The main town, Chora, beckons with its white-washed buildings adorned with colorful bougainvillaeas. Meander through its narrow pathways, where every corner seems to hold a new discovery.

Day 6: Folegandros' Tranquility

Today is an ode to tranquility as you discover Folegandros' secluded beaches. Agios Nikolaos and Livadaki, nestled in hidden coves, offer a serene escape from the world. Sink your toes into the soft sands, dip into the crystal-clear waters, and relish the privacy and peace that these hidden shores provide.

As the sun begins its descent, position yourself to witness the Aegean embrace the golden hues of twilight. Capture the island's raw beauty in the waning light, a moment to be preserved in memory and photographs alike. The calmness of Folegandros serves as the perfect backdrop for a serene sunset, bidding farewell to another day in the Cyclades.

Day 7: Farewell to Cyclades

With a heart full of memories and experiences, it's time to bid farewell to this Cycladic adventure. Return to Santorini for your departure, where the spirit of ancient history and cultural exploration accompanies you on your journey home. As you leave the Cyclades, carry with you the warmth of its sunsets, the echoes of its legends, and the magic of its islands that will forever remain etched in your soul.

# Itinerary 3: Adventure and Nature Exploration

### Day 1: Arrival in Milos

As you step off the ferry onto the shores of Milos, a sense of anticipation fills the air. Milos is a Cycladic gem known for its diverse landscapes and hidden coves, ready to unveil its wonders to you. The island's charm lies not only in its pristine beaches but also in its unique geological formations and cultural riches. After settling into your accommodation and taking in the sea breeze, your adventure begins.

Exploring Plaka: The Enchanting Capital

Head to Plaka, the island's picturesque capital perched on a hill overlooking the Aegean Sea. The narrow cobblestone streets lead you through a labyrinth of white-washed houses adorned with vibrant bougainvillaeas. Discover charming boutiques, local crafts, and art galleries that showcase the island's creative spirit.

Indulge in a Traditional Greek Dinner

As the sun begins to set, find a cozy taverna nestled within Plaka's alleys. Delight in a traditional Greek dinner that tantalizes your taste buds with flavors of olive oil, fresh herbs, and local ingredients. Savor dishes like moussaka, souvlaki, and feta-stuffed phyllo pastry, surrounded by the warmth of Greek hospitality.

**Day 2: Milos' Natural Wonders**

Rendezvous with Sarakiniko Beach

Today, you venture to Sarakiniko Beach, a place that seems to belong to another world. Its lunar landscape, sculpted by volcanic activity, presents a surreal setting of white volcanic rocks contrasted against the deep blue sea. Wander through the labyrinth of smooth rocks and find hidden coves that invite you for a refreshing swim.

Boat Tour to Kleftiko Caves

In the afternoon, embark on a boat tour to the legendary Kleftiko Caves. These sea caves, once a pirate hideout, offer an awe-inspiring spectacle of turquoise waters and towering rock formations. Dive into the crystal-clear waters and explore the underwater beauty, as your boat captain regales you with tales of the past.

**Day 3: Sifnos Serenity**

Ferry to Tranquil Sifnos

Board the ferry to Sifnos, a serene island that embraces a slower pace of life and focuses on preserving its traditional culture and cuisine. As you arrive at the harbor, the calm atmosphere instantly embraces you, inviting you to unwind and embrace the island's authenticity.

Discovering Apollonia's Pottery Village

Head to Apollonia, the island's main town, known for its charming streets and squares. A highlight is the pottery village, where you can witness the intricate process of crafting traditional ceramics. Stroll through the workshops, interact with local artisans, and perhaps even find a unique keepsake to take home.

**Day 4: Hiking and Relaxation in Sifnos**

Ascending to Profitis Ilias Monastery

Today's adventure leads you to the heights of Sifnos as you embark on a hike to the Profitis Ilias Monastery. The trail winds through picturesque landscapes, offering panoramic views of the island's rolling hills and sparkling sea. Upon reaching the monastery, the panoramic vistas that unfold before you are nothing short of breathtaking.

Beach Bliss at Vathi or Platys Gialos

After the invigorating hike, treat yourself to a leisurely afternoon on the golden sands of Vathi Beach or Platys Gialos Beach. Sink your toes into the soft sand, swim in the inviting waters, and bask in the gentle Mediterranean sun. As the day draws to a close, relish the sense of tranquility that defines Sifnos.

## Day 5: Serifos Exploration

Journey to Undiscovered Serifos

Today, you set sail for Serifos, an off-the-beaten-path gem that promises untouched beauty and an authentic island atmosphere. As the ferry docks in the harbor, you'll instantly feel the island's raw charm. Serifos offers a quieter Cycladic experience, where nature's majesty takes center stage.

Exploring Chora: The Heart of Serifos

Stroll through Chora, Serifos' main town, where white-washed buildings cascade down the hillside. Wander the winding streets, discover local shops, and take in the views from the castle ruins. Chora's simplicity and unspoiled architecture transport you back in time, allowing you to truly immerse yourself in the island's authentic character.

## Day 6: Serifos' Outdoor Adventures

Hiking to Monastery of Taxiarches

Today's adventure leads you on a hike to the Monastery of Taxiarches, situated high on a hill overlooking the island. As you ascend the rocky trail, the landscape unfolds in all its glory, revealing rugged terrain and breathtaking vistas. Upon reaching the monastery, you're rewarded with not only the sense of accomplishment but also the opportunity to soak in the serenity that surrounds you.

Discovering Livadakia Beach

In the afternoon, make your way to Livadakia Beach, a pristine crescent of golden sands kissed by the azure waters. Whether you choose to swim, snorkel, or simply relax by the shore, Livadakia offers a picturesque setting to unwind and reflect on the adventures of your journey.

## Day 7: Farewell to Cyclades

Reflecting on the Journey

As your week-long adventure in the Cyclades comes to an end, return to Milos to bid farewell to this enchanting archipelago. Take a moment to reflect on the memories you've created, the natural wonders you've witnessed, and the authentic experiences that have enriched your journey.

Departure with Memories

Whether you're leaving from Milos' harbor or its airport, depart with a heart full of gratitude for the captivating beauty of the Cyclades. The landscapes, culture, and adventures you've encountered will forever remain a part of you, inspiring future travels and reminding you of the magic that exists within these Aegean islands.

These itineraries offer just a glimpse of the countless possibilities for a 7-day adventure in the Cyclades. Whether you're seeking beaches, history, or outdoor exploration, the Cycladic islands are sure to captivate your heart and leave you with unforgettable memories of your journey through this enchanting archipelago.

# Chapter 7: Practical Tips and Travel Essentials

Traveling to the Cyclades is a thrilling experience, but it's important to be prepared with essential knowledge and information that will make your journey smooth, safe, and enjoyable. This chapter covers practical tips and travel essentials that every visitor should be aware of before embarking on their Cyclades adventure.

## Currency, Language, and Communication

Currency: The official currency in Greece is the Euro (€). ATMs are widely available on most islands, and credit cards are generally accepted in larger establishments. However, it's advisable to carry some cash, especially when exploring smaller villages or markets where card payments might not be as common.

Language: The official language is Greek, but due to the popularity of the Cyclades among tourists, many locals in popular tourist areas speak English. It's still helpful to learn a few basic Greek phrases as a gesture of respect and to enhance your interactions with locals.

Communication: Mobile phone coverage is generally good on the main islands, but it might be spotty in more remote areas. If you plan to use your phone extensively, consider purchasing a local SIM card with a data plan to stay connected. Additionally, public Wi-Fi is available in cafes, restaurants, and some hotels, but don't rely solely on it for important communications.

## Staying Safe and Healthy: Medical Facilities and Precautions

Health Precautions: Before traveling to the Cyclades, consult your doctor about necessary vaccinations and health precautions. The sun can be intense in the region, so pack sunscreen, sunglasses, and a hat to protect yourself from sunburn. Stay hydrated, especially during hot summer months.

Healthcare: The larger islands, such as Santorini, Mykonos, and Naxos, have medical facilities and pharmacies that can provide basic medical assistance. However, for serious medical issues, you might need to be transferred to the mainland. It's wise to have travel insurance that covers medical emergencies.

Emergency Services: The emergency number in Greece is 112. This number connects you to police, medical services, and fire departments.

Staying Safe: The Cyclades are generally safe for travelers. However, it's always a good idea to take common-sense precautions like safeguarding your belongings, avoiding poorly lit or isolated areas at night, and being cautious when swimming in unfamiliar waters.

# Responsible Travel: Navigating Environmental Concerns

Environmental Awareness: The Cyclades' stunning natural beauty is a major draw for visitors, and it's crucial to help preserve this environment. Avoid leaving any trash behind, and be sure to dispose of waste responsibly in designated bins. Some islands have recycling programs, so be mindful of separating your waste if possible.

Water Conservation: Water scarcity can be an issue on certain islands, especially during the dry summer months. Conserve water whenever possible by taking shorter showers and reusing towels in accommodations that promote sustainability.

Respecting Local Culture: The Cyclades have a rich cultural heritage, and it's important to respect local customs and traditions. When visiting religious sites or monasteries, dress modestly and adhere to any guidelines provided. Keep in mind that some businesses and attractions might close during siesta hours, which are typically in the early afternoon.

Supporting Local Economy: Opt for locally owned accommodations, restaurants, and shops to contribute to the local economy and community. This allows you to have a more authentic experience and connect with the island's culture.

Protecting Marine Life: If you're engaging in water activities like snorkeling or diving, be mindful of the marine life and coral reefs. Avoid touching or damaging coral, and never remove marine organisms from their natural habitat.

As you prepare for your Cyclades adventure, these practical tips and travel essentials will serve as invaluable tools for a smooth and enjoyable trip. By understanding the local currency, language, and communication options, staying informed about health precautions, and embracing responsible travel practices, you'll not only have a wonderful experience but also contribute positively to the preservation of the Cyclades' natural beauty and cultural heritage. With these insights, you're ready to embark on a journey that will create lasting memories and a deep appreciation for this remarkable Greek island paradise.

# Chapter 8: Saying Farewell to the Cyclades

As your journey through the enchanting Cyclades archipelago draws to a close, it's natural to reflect on the incredible experiences and memories you've gathered along the way. This final chapter serves as a moment of contemplation and practical guidance, helping you make the transition from the idyllic islands back to reality.

**Reflections on Your Cycladic Adventure**

As you bid adieu to the Cyclades, take some time to reflect on the unique moments and emotions that have colored your travel experience. Whether you've been captivated by the stunning sunsets over Santorini's caldera, charmed by the labyrinthine streets of Mykonos, or humbled by the historical richness of Naxos, each island holds a piece of your heart. Consider jotting down your thoughts in a travel journal, capturing the essence of your journey through words and sketches.

Think about the connections you've made with fellow travelers and locals, the flavors that have delighted your taste buds, and the landscapes that have taken your breath away. Remember the laughter shared on the beaches, the awe-inspired moments at ancient ruins, and the quiet contemplation as you gazed out at the Aegean Sea. These reflections will not only serve as cherished mementos but will also enrich your memories as time goes on.

## Packing Up and Checking Out: Departure Logistics

As you prepare to leave the Cyclades, there are a few practical steps to consider for a smooth departure. Here's a checklist to guide you through the process:

- Check-Out from Accommodation: Ensure you settle any outstanding bills, return keys or access cards, and express your gratitude to the staff for their hospitality. Many hotels and guesthouses offer luggage storage facilities, which can be handy if you have a few hours to spare before your departure.

- Review Your Itinerary: Double-check your transportation arrangements. Make sure you have your ferry or flight tickets, along with any necessary reservations, printed out or accessible on your phone. Timetables can change, so it's a good idea to verify departure times a day in advance.

- Pack Thoughtfully: Revisit your packing list and ensure you haven't left any personal items behind. Be considerate of the environment by disposing of waste responsibly and recycling when possible.

- Souvenirs and Gifts: If you've collected souvenirs or gifts during your journey, pack them securely to prevent damage. Consider leaving space in your luggage for these items or use additional bags if needed.

- Travel Documents: Keep your passport, identification, travel insurance details, and any important documents in a secure and easily accessible place.

- Last-Minute Explorations: If you have a few hours before departure, consider spending some time in a local café, revisiting a favorite spot, or taking a leisurely stroll to soak in the ambiance one last time.

- Saying Goodbye: Take a moment to bid farewell to the islands. Capture a few final photos to commemorate your adventure and perhaps write a message in your travel journal that encapsulates your feelings as you say goodbye.

- Transport to the Port/Airport: Plan your transport to the port or airport in advance. Taxis, buses, and private shuttles are often readily available, but it's wise to allow extra time in case of unexpected delays.

- Embrace Wanderlust: As you leave the Cyclades, remember that this chapter is just one part of your travel story. The experiences you've gained and the memories you've created will continue to inspire your wanderlust for future adventures.

Departing from the Cyclades can be bittersweet, but the memories you've gathered will remain with you forever. As you journey back to reality, carry the spirit of the islands with you, knowing that the beauty, culture, and tranquility of the Cyclades will always be a part of your travel tapestry.

# Appendix: Handy Resources and References

When embarking on your Cyclades adventure, having access to useful websites, travel apps, and local knowledge can greatly enhance your experience. This appendix provides a curated list of valuable resources to help you make the most of your journey through the enchanting Cycladic islands.

## Useful Websites, Apps, and Travel Services:

FerryHopper: A comprehensive online platform that allows you to plan, compare, and book ferry tickets for your island-hopping adventure. The user-friendly interface provides real-time schedules, availability, and prices, ensuring smooth transitions between the Cyclades islands.

Visit Greece Official Website: The official website of the Greek National Tourism Organization offers a wealth of information on the Cyclades, including destination guides, travel tips, and cultural insights. It's a reliable source for up-to-date details on attractions, accommodations, and events.

Google Maps: An essential tool for navigating the Cyclades, Google Maps provides directions, distance estimations, and street views. Download maps for offline use to avoid data charges while exploring the islands.

Weather Apps: Apps like AccuWeather, The Weather Channel, or local Greek weather apps provide accurate forecasts, helping you plan outdoor activities and pack appropriately for your journey.

XE Currency Converter: As you hop from island to island, having a reliable currency converter app can help you stay on top of local currencies, exchange rates, and budgeting.

Couchsurfing and Airbnb: These platforms offer diverse accommodation options, from staying with locals to renting unique properties. They can add a personalized touch to your Cyclades experience.

Google Translate: While English is widely spoken in tourist areas, having a language translation app can be helpful for communicating with locals and understanding signs and menus.

Travel Forums and Blogs: Websites like TripAdvisor, Lonely Planet's Thorn Tree Forum, and travel blogs provide insights and firsthand experiences shared by fellow travelers. They can offer valuable advice on hidden gems, dining recommendations, and more.

# Glossary of Local Terms and Phrases:

Immerse yourself in the local culture by familiarizing yourself with some common Greek terms and phrases. While English is widely understood, using a few Greek words can go a long way in connecting with locals and showing your appreciation for their culture.

- Kalimera: Good morning
- Kalispera: Good evening
- Efharisto: Thank you
- Parakalo: Please/You're welcome
- Nai: Yes
- Ohi: No
- Yamas: Cheers
- Poli orea: Very beautiful
- Ta leme: Goodbye
- Pame: Let's go
- Ena, dio, tria: One, two, three
- To parakato: The bill, please
- Pame gia kafe: Let's go for coffee
- Poso kanei auto?: How much does this cost?
- Pou einai i paralia?: Where is the beach?

Using these phrases can enhance your interactions with locals and create memorable moments as you explore the Cyclades islands.

When visiting the Cyclades, having a reliable language translation app can greatly enhance your travel experience, especially if you want to communicate with locals, read signs, and understand menus. Here are five popular language translation apps that can be incredibly useful during your journey:

- Google Translate: Google Translate is one of the most well-known and widely used translation apps. It supports translations between a vast number of languages and offers features like text translation, voice translation, and even camera translation. You can take a picture of text (like a menu) and have it translated in real time.

- iTranslate: iTranslate is a user-friendly app that offers translations in over 100 languages. It provides text and voice translations, as well as the ability to save and organize your favorite phrases. The app also offers a handy "AirTranslate" feature for seamless communication between devices.

- Microsoft Translator: Microsoft Translator is another robust translation app with features like text translation, voice translation, and camera translation. One standout feature is the "Conversation Mode," which allows two people to have a bilingual conversation using the app, making it great for interacting with locals.

- TripLingo: TripLingo is designed specifically for travelers and offers not only language translation but also cultural tips, essential phrases, and even a built-in voice translator. It also provides a "slang slider" that adjusts the level of formality in translations, so you can communicate in a way that feels appropriate.

- Papago: Developed by Naver, a South Korean tech company, Papago is an excellent translation app for Asian languages, which can be particularly useful if you're traveling from Asia to the Cyclades. It supports languages like Korean, Japanese, Chinese, and more, making it a great choice for tourists from these regions.

Before your trip, make sure to download the necessary language packs for offline use, especially if you might find yourself in areas with limited or no internet connectivity. These translation apps can be a lifeline for effective communication and a deeper understanding of the local culture during your time in the Cyclades.

Made in United States
Troutdale, OR
09/04/2023